JIMMY
STEWART
A Wonderful Life

JIMMY STEWART

A Wonderful Life

Jonathan Coe

ARCADE PUBLISHING · NEW YORK

PICTURE SOURCES
Aquarius 80, 107, 121, 125 *top*, 139, 161, 188
Ronald Grant Archive 33, 91, 128, 143, 168, 172, 174, 187
Hulton-Deutsch Collection 13, 40 *top*, 77 *top*, 78, 79, 102, 149, 184 *bottom*
Imperial War Museum 75 *bottom,* 76
Katz/Snap 16 *top*, 21, 64, 106
Kobal Collection, 2, 8, 10, 11, 12, 14, 26, 28, 28-9, 34, 35, 48, 49, 41, 42, 47, 48, 51, 52, 52-3, 59, 61, 65, 66, 70, 71 *top*, 72, 83, 86, 87, 888, 92, 92, 93, 95, 96, 97, 99, 101, 104, 109, 111, 113, 118, 119, 123, 124, 129, 132, 134-5, 140, 151, 152, 158, 160, 162, 165, 167, 173, 176, 177, 183, 184 *top*, 185 *bottom*, 189
Moviestore 27 *bottom*, 36, 84, 85, 116, 125 *bottom*, 147, 185 *top*
New York Public Library 23
Pictorial Press 25, 32, 69 *bottom*, 71 *bottom*, 73, 82, 105, 130, 169, 171, 182
Popperfoto 75 *top*
Princeton University Library 18-19, 19, 20

Picture Research by Anne-Marie Ehrlich

Arcade Publishing books may be purchased in bulk at special discounts for sales promotion, corporate gifts, fund-raising, or educational purposes. Special editions can also be created to specifications. For details, contact the Special Sales Department, Arcade Publishing, 307 West 36th Street, 11th Floor, New York, NY 10018 or arcade@skyhorsepublishing.com.

Arcade Publishing® is a registered trademark of Skyhorse Publishing, Inc.®, a Delaware corporation.

Visit our website at www.arcadepub.com.

10 9 8 7 6 5 4 3 2 1

Library of Congress Cataloging-in-Publication Data is available.
ISBN: 978-1-61145-712-4

Printed in China

For my parents

ACKNOWLEDGMENTS

In these days of VCRs and satellite dishes everyone has become a film archivist, and I would like to thank Julian Knott, Jenny Cheshire, Malcolm Daintry and Chris Stevens for supplying me with copies of hard-to-find films. Thanks also to the staff of the BFI Library and Viewing Services for their constant helpfulness.

Contents

INTRODUCTION

James Stewart should be approached with care; perhaps even with reverence. Few other actors have been held in such esteem within their own profession, or in such affection by the public. Andrew Sarris famously labelled Stewart 'the most complete actor-personality in the American cinema'; David Thomson got closer to the secret of his appeal by calling him 'one of the most trusted of American actors'; while for Robert Horton, the truth is even starker: Stewart may quite possibly be 'America's most beloved man'.

Curiously, much of that love continues to centre upon a myth – upon the figure of the incorruptible American patriot, a part that Stewart in fact played only a handful of times and which is crystallised in a film now more than fifty years old. But the implications of Frank Capra's *Mr Smith Goes to Washington* have reverberated throughout his career. A glance at the names of some of Stewart's characters bears this out: Jefferson Smith became Thomas Jefferson Destry, who became Tom Jeffords who became Jeff Webster; and then there was Bill Smith and Lawrence Smith – to say nothing of Bill Lawrence. Stewart has been happy to assume the rôle of America's Everyman in his public life, and happy to reprise variations of it in film after film; but what needs to be emphasised is how extreme and complex some of those variations were.

It detracts nothing from Stewart's integrity, in other words, to point out that his screen career is actually riddled with contradictions. He was a stalwart of Hollywood's 'Golden Age' who rose through the ranks when the studio system was at its height, but even in his earliest films he gave performances that nowadays seem strikingly modern in technique. Cary Grant, with whom he acted only once, expressed this very clearly when he remarked, 'Cyclically speaking, Jimmy Stewart had the same effect on pictures that Marlon Brando

Relaxing on the set during the shooting of NO HIGHWAY.

had some years later. Jimmy had the ability to talk naturally. He knew that in conversations people *do* often interrupt one another and that it's not always so easy to get a thought out. It took a little while for the sound men to get used to him, but he had an *enormous* impact. And then, some years later, Marlon came out and did the same thing all over again – but what people forget is that Jimmy did it first.'

Then there is the question of Stewart's politics, and how they have frequently gone against the grain of his acting career. His lifelong Republicanism, impressed upon him very firmly by his parents, but then tempered by the liberalism of his closest friends in the 1930s (Henry Fonda, Josh Logan, Burgess Meredith), has solidified and grown ever more inflexible over the years. Now and again it has flared up in his films – few people would regret the loss of *Strategic Air Command* or *The FBI Story*, I suspect – but what's more interesting is how fully he has been prepared to commit himself to projects that never sat very comfortably with his own values. Thus he has made pacifist statements in *Shenandoah*, undermined the very basis of the Old West in *The Man Who Shot Liberty Valance* and has even, in *Mr Smith* itself (not that he or Capra ever realised it), drawn damaging attention to loopholes in the capitalist system. You might say that the only one of his films to do lasting harm in the political arena was *The Stratton Story*; and that was because Ronald Reagan was so mortified when Stewart landed the starring part, snatching it from under his nose, that he decided to give up acting altogether and devote himself full-time to the Republican cause.

On the set of IT'S A WONDERFUL LIFE.

Bing Crosby – soon to co-star with Grace Kelly in HIGH SOCIETY *– visits the* REAR WINDOW *set.*

In 1934 Hedda Hopper urged Stewart to come to Hollywood by insisting that 'the movies need someone as clean and sincere as you'. There will always be a hard core of admirers who persist in finding him reductively wholesome, who see in him nothing more than the cinematic equivalent of Mom's apple pie (whose virtues he really does hymn in *The Shopworn Angel*). But many of Stewart's key performances – whether he likes it or not – are subversive of this image: *It's a Wonderful Life* shows that small-town cosiness can only be bought at a terrible personal cost; *Harvey* argues that alcohol-induced euphoria is preferable to family life; the Anthony Mann Westerns uncover violence and neurosis at the heart of the cowboy hero; and *Vertigo* suggests that male desire, the bedrock of American family values, is founded upon a tragic obsession with manipulation and control. In lending himself to these extraordinary films, Stewart somehow managed to retain the loyalty of his mainstream audience while willingly putting himself further out on a limb than any comparable actor of his generation.

Stewart enjoyed pushing himself to extremes, both by testing the limits of his physical prowess (as Anthony Mann has testified) and by actively hunting out rôles that would stretch him as an actor. After *Vertigo*, fewer and fewer dramatic challenges came his way, but the body of work he had established by then puts the seriousness of his achievement beyond question. Gore Vidal once described himself – with characteristic modesty – as America's biographer, but the most plausible claim to this title could be made for James Stewart. Taken as a whole, his seventy-nine feature films constitute America's definitive screen biography, and in presenting the many faces of the country he loves so dearly he has revealed it to be a far more troubled, likeable, fractured, dark, complex, funny and *human* place than we might otherwise ever have thought possible.

Posing with Hitchcock, who was to become one of his favourite directors.

1

THE IDEAL WAY TO MAKE PICTURES
1908-1938

Frank Capra was the director who made the first decisive intervention in James Stewart's career. Watching Stewart's dignified, affecting performance in MGM's starchy 1937 flagwaver, *Navy Blue and Gold*, he recognised a valuable asset, one that had not so far been exploited by the directors who had presided over the aimless competence of Stewart's first dozen or so films, but which Capra himself would soon set about deploying to his own political and cinematic ends. What he saw, in short, was a unique combination of qualities: 'I sensed the character and rock-ribbed honesty of a Gary Cooper, plus the breeding and intelligence of an Ivy League idealist.'

It's the second of these qualities that has tended to get overlooked in the fog of mythology surrounding the stories of Stewart's folksy, small-town background. The family into which he was born, on 20 May 1908, was a wealthy, conservative and educated one. The Stewarts had arrived from Ireland and established themselves in the town of Indiana, Pennsylvania, at the close of the eighteenth century. Some fifty years later, Stewart's grandfather founded the town's hardware store. Ramshackle and quaint though this enterprise has been made to sound over the years (in the course of numerous interviews), it must have developed into an extremely profitable family business; there was enough money around, for instance, to send Stewart's father Alexander to Princeton, to put his children through private school, and, in 1914, to move the family into a two-storey house at 104 North Seventh Street which still looks fairly imposing today.

By all accounts Alexander, who inherited the store, appears to have run it along unorthodox lines, sometimes preferring to barter rather than accept payment in cash. (A fact that in itself suggests he was not exactly desperate for

Stewart with his mother, Elizabeth: the earliest surviving photograph.

funds.) A travelling circus passing through town is reported to have paid for its goods with a twelve-foot python, which was put in the shop window and fed live mice by the seven-year-old Stewart. More significantly, another item that came into the store in lieu of payment was an old accordion; it was passed on to Stewart and he learned to play it, an accomplishment that would stand him in good stead at the outset of his dramatic career.

The atmosphere in the Stewart household seems to have been energetic, boisterous and informal; Stewart has spoken of his father being 'pugnacious and gay, full of a thirst for adventure', and one is irresistibly reminded of the noisy, life-loving Bailey family in the early scenes of Capra's *It's a Wonderful Life*. Their dynamism and confidence, however, had a firm grounding in conservative values. The Stewarts were dutiful members of the First Presbyterian Church of Indiana, and fervent patriots with a long history of military involvement. Stewart's great-great-grandfather fought in the Revolutionary War, and since then, in the words of a childhood friend, Bill Moorhead, 'there has been a Stewart in every American war: it didn't matter if they were under weight or over age – somehow they managed to find ways to serve their country'. Stewart's mother recalled that when Alexander enlisted to fight in World War I (at the age of forty-six), the young Jimmy persuaded her to buy him a miniature soldier suit, which he wore constantly while his father was away and would not even allow her to wash. Echoes of this early fetish for all things military can be noticed in the happiness and sense of ease that would later beam out of Stewart's face whenever he got to wear a uniform on screen – as, for example, in *Born to Dance*, *Shopworn Angel*, *The Glenn Miller Story* and *Strategic Air Command*.

Among the more frequently repeated anecdotes dating from this period are the stories of how Stewart nearly killed himself, at the age of four, by tying a box kite to his go-cart and attempting to fly it from the roof of the house; how he staged amateur dramatic productions in his parents' basement (patriotic affairs, naturally, with titles like *The Slacker* and *To Hell with the Kaiser*) and how he later assisted as a projectionist at the local cinema during his school holidays. Tempting though it may be to see these as pointers towards his future career and lifelong interest in aviation, it seems equally truthful to say that they sound like the more or less typical enthusiasms of any resourceful, imaginative young boy growing up in such a time and place. Stewart has said that he 'can't recall anything unpleasant' from his childhood, and this implies that there was rarely any painful conflict with the parental values which dictated, among other things, that his schooling should take place at Mercersburg Academy, a local private boarding school steeped in Presbyterian ritual and tradition. Similarly, he deferred to his father's wishes at the end of his prep-school years, when it came to the choice of college: Stewart himself favoured the Naval Academy in Annapolis, but Alexander wanted him to go to Princeton, of which he had fond memories from his own student days.

As it turned out, the move to Princeton was a very fortuitous one. Not that Stewart had now found his feet academically: he began as an engineering major (but couldn't cope with calculus), switched to political science (but found that his reading speeds weren't up to it) and finally studied architecture, in which he graduated with honours. His extra-curricular activities at Princeton, however, would signal the discovery of his true vocation. Whereas at Mercersburg he had directed most of his energies towards the track and football teams, with a token appearance in the class play *The Wolves* somehow squeezed in along the way, at Princeton these priorities would be reversed. Finding his lanky build more and more of a liability on the football field, Stewart turned increasingly to drama, and was one of more than two hundred hopefuls who auditioned for Princeton's famous theatre group, the Triangle Club. He performed a not very distinguished audition piece – the director apparently had trouble adjusting to his softly-spoken mannerisms – but was recruited anyway, mainly on the strength of his accordion-playing.

Although Stewart also belonged to another student group, Théâtre Intime, which specialised in serious drama, he was clearly more at home in the

Triangle productions – light-hearted affairs with an emphasis on music and undergraduate humour. They would open on campus and then go on tour across the country, often attracting a good deal of attention from the Hollywood and Broadway talent scouts. Stewart took only minor parts in his first two years, and his contributions were predominantly musical. His singing voice has always been excellent (it can be heard to best advantage in MGM's *Born to Dance*) and he even cut a record as lead vocalist at this time, on a song called 'Love Comes But Once', which was written by his fellow student José Ferrer and performed by his band The Pied Pipers. It was while performing a musical number entitled 'Blue Hell' in the 1928 Triangle production, *The Golden Dog*, that Stewart was spotted by the writer and star of the show, Josh Logan. Logan was taken by the 'attractive personality' that Stewart projected on stage, but recalled that when he asked the incipient architect whether he

On stage (seated, far right) in the Théâtre Intime production of NERISSA, *1930.*

had ever considered becoming a professional actor, he simply turned on his heel and 'walked away as if I had slandered him'. Two years later, however, Logan would write an entire show specifically with Stewart in mind. It was called *The Tiger Smiles*, and won its leading actor a favourable review and a picture in *Time* magazine. Stewart's leisurely, naturalistic delivery and (perhaps calculated) air of amateurism made a very favourable impression upon audiences. 'He spoke in a stately pavane even then,' Logan has written. 'He still felt he was an architect. This stage "monkey business" was just fun. But he was so good I knew deep down he loved acting but was too embarrassed to admit it.'

Stewart, Josh Logan (centre) and Marshall Dana in the 1930 Triangle Club production, THE TIGER SMILES.

Prior to writing this show, Logan had been involved in setting up a theatre group called the University Players, which was based at a movie theatre in West Falmouth on Cape Cod, Massachusetts. Conceived as a collaborative venture between Princeton's Théâtre Intime and the Harvard Dramatic Society, it soon expanded to include performers from Smith, Yale, Vassar and Radcliffe. In its brief existence (from July 1928 to November 1932) it built up an impressive reputation, and several of its members went on to successful Hollywood careers – notably Henry Fonda, Myron McCormick and Margaret Sullavan. The troupe was youthful, idealistic and highly volatile. 'We were totally involved, ecstatically alive,' according to Logan, who also observed, rather more coolly, 'The energy of two dozen undiscovered stars, the mixture of grand and poor, mostly poor, the fact that everyone was nearly the same age, the lack of a principal or teacher to shake fingers or teach "academic precepts" – all of this made for a kind of hell ... Physical fights were non-existent, but belligerent stand-offs could last for days.'

One of these 'belligerent stand-offs' lasted for more than days – lasted for good, in fact – when Henry Fonda left the group in 1932, citing 'discontent at the way the University Players was being run'. Thus the Players had a vacancy for a leading man at the very time Stewart was graduating from Princeton. At this point, none the less, a career on stage or in the cinema was still very far from his mind. Even though the Depression was now at its height and there was little chance that he would find immediate employment with an architectural firm, his preferred options were either to go home and work in the family business, or to stay on at Princeton and pursue a graduate studies programme, for which he had already been awarded a scholarship. A few months spent at Falmouth with Logan and friends would merely be an agreeable little prelude to one or other of these more sober courses.

With Josh Logan in Falmouth, Massachusetts (1932).

That summer, in any case, he was to find himself witnessing the last, rancorous days of the University Players. After scoring two modest successes with a Booth Tarkington comedy, *Magnolia* (in which Stewart was 'howlingly funny'), and Lawrence E. Johnston's *It's a Wild Child* (where Stewart proved himself, in Logan's view, to be 'a fine actor – honest and talented'), the Players allowed themselves to be seduced by promises of Broadway exposure into ceding control over their affairs to a New York producer, Arthur J. Beckhard. His pet project was a lumbering biographical melodrama about a temperance campaigner, Frank McGrath's *Carry Nation*, with his wife (a singer, not an actress) in the leading rôle. Described by Logan as 'a groaning bore' in its Falmouth run, the play opened at New York's Biltmore Theater in October 1932, marking James Stewart's Broadway début in no fewer than four bit parts. It was poorly reviewed, and closed after only thirty-one performances. Morale among the performers had collapsed to a fatal low, and the company broke up.

Stewart, who had only been with the players a few months and hadn't made much of an emotional investment in the venture, was by now quite prepared to pack up and go home, not especially

In swashbuckling vein for the Triangle Club production Spanish Blades *(1931).*

downhearted. But Beckhard quickly made amends by finding a part for him – and for many of the other cast members – in a comedy called *Goodbye Again*, which opened in December 1932 and turned out to be a long-running hit. Although Stewart's rôle was only a three-minute cameo (for which he was paid $35 a week), it regularly brought the house down and the move back to Indiana was postponed. He, Logan and Myron McCormick moved into an apartment on West 63rd Street and after a while, in a generous display of hatchet-burying, they were joined by Henry Fonda – now unemployed, impoverished and reeling from his short-lived marriage to Margaret Sullavan.

On Broadway with Sally Bates in GOODBYE AGAIN *(1932): the acting bug was beginning to bite.*

Fonda christened the apartment 'Casa Gangrene'. There was one twin-bedded bedroom, a living room with two couches, a damp and evil-smelling bathroom, and a large kitchen stove out in the hallway. Most of the other tenants in the building were prostitutes and, according to legend, the gangster Legs Diamond lived in a hotel two doors up the street. Every so often, said Fonda, 'We'd be sitting there, after the theater, drinking a beer or two and the door would open. We'd turn around and three characters that looked like they'd just walked in from a Warner Brothers gangster movie would appear: Chesterfield coats with black velvet collars up and white Borsalino hats pulled down, dark glasses, and hands in their pockets; they'd walk over to the bedroom, glance around, shrug, never open their mouths, and leave.'

Ironically it was Fonda, the most experienced actor of the four and at this point the most versatile, who was finding it hardest to rustle up any work, while Stewart, with his take-it-or-leave-it attitude to the profession, rarely seemed to be out of a job. Occasionally he worked as a stage manager, but more often he would get by on small, undemanding parts in minor plays which, if he was lucky, would stagger through runs of a month or two. And although he may have told himself that this hand-to-mouth Broadway existence was 'all some kind of big mistake – not like I'd planned at all', a sense of momentum was gradually beginning to build. In March 1934 he landed the meaty part of Sergeant O'Hara, a young Marine who volunteers to test a possible cure for yellow fever, in Sidney Howard's *Yellow Jack*, and this not only brought him to the attention of MGM talent scout Bill Grady, but also provided a sense of fulfilment which had been lacking from his earlier, more frivolous rôles. Logan had by now spotted a change in his friend: 'The theater was fast becoming the sole ambition of his life.' Or, as Fonda put it, Stewart at this point 'took a long,

slow look around him and at himself and began to think maybe he'd blundered into something pretty good'.

It was only a matter of time before the movies claimed him. He had his first experience in front of the cameras during the summer of 1934, when he took a small part in *Art Trouble*, a Warner Brothers comedy short shot in New York. Then, on the recommendation of Hedda Hopper, with whom he had appeared on Broadway in *Divided by Three*, he was given the latest in a series of screen tests by MGM. Eventually, in June 1935, Bill Grady summoned him to Hollywood to take sixth billing in *The Murder Man*, MGM's first starring vehicle for their new acquisition from Fox, Spencer Tracy. Stewart's performance as a newspaper reporter called Shorty passed without comment, and it was some months before the studio (which had put him under short-term contract at $350 a week) bothered to use him again.

Henry Fonda had made the transition to Hollywood, too, so it was natural that he and Stewart should continue to live together. They rented a house in Brentwood, where they were joined by another ex-University Player, John Swope, and, a few weeks later, by Josh Logan, who had been hired as voice coach on Selznick's ill-fated Marlene Dietrich movie, *The Garden of Allah*. In many ways it meant a resumption of their carefree, rather innocent New York lifestyle; Fonda and Stewart, for instance, spent much of their spare time making model aeroplanes, which does not exactly square with the popular image of Hollywood as Sin City. But there were a couple of important differences – namely, that they were surrounded by some of the most famous people in America (their next-door neighbour was Greta Garbo, although she remained well hidden behind an eight-foot fence) and, more importantly, that they were now making at least ten times as much money.

After his shaky start in *The Murder Man*, Stewart began to climb up the MGM star roster with surprising agility. The parts were not always well chosen, but at least constituted a busy apprenticeship which would enable him to piece together – if somewhat haphazardly – the elements of a distinctive screen personality. A supporting rôle as Jeanette MacDonald's wayward brother in the 1936 remake of *Rose Marie* did him no harm at all: his brief scenes of contrition at the end of the picture give it a welcome touch of realism. And following that, he was loaned to Universal and found that he had been miraculously promoted to co-star in what was only his third feature film.

The good fairy behind this unexpected turn of events was Margaret Sullavan, who would go on to make four films with Stewart, including two of his finest. Since her days with the University Players her career had blossomed against all odds; despite a series of failed marriages (she was the wife, in rapid succession, of Fonda, director William Wyler and agent Leland Hayward) and a reputation for being temperamental which derived from nothing more than her own chronic insecurity, two of her films, *Only Yesterday* and *Little Man, What Now?*, had already proved hugely popular with both critics and audiences. Although Sullavan and Stewart had in fact never acted together before, her friendship with him went back to Princeton where, as a leading light of the University Players, she had been imported as guest star for a Théâtre Intime production of *The Artist and the Lady*, on which Stewart had worked as stage manager. They dated at the time, and it seems likely that Stewart continued to carry a torch for

A boyish-looking Stewart at a party given by Jeanette MacDonald and Gene Raymond (both seated, with Nelson Eddy).

Suffering nobly in NEXT TIME WE LOVE, with Margaret Sullavan.

her afterwards: some even maintain that it was because of his passion for Sullavan that he remained unmarried until his forties. Whatever the truth of the matter, she insisted upon Stewart as co-star for her fifth film, *Next Time We Love*, and here, as in their other collaborations, there was a quiet, perceptible, somewhat exclusive intimacy between them on screen. But the film itself, sadly, was all too typical of the shameless tearjerkers which studio bosses, apparently blind to Sullavan's comic gifts and aura of melancholy intelligence, would insist on building around her. She plays a Broadway actress, Cicely Tyler, torn between her dramatic ambitions and the desire to follow her reporter husband (Stewart) on a special assignment to Rome. After numerous tearful parting scenes we are treated to a tragic climax in which it is disclosed, to cap it all, that Stewart has a fatal illness. Understandably, the actor looks ill at ease with this material and *Variety* chastised him for a performance made up largely of 'a series of behaviorisms that frequently make neither rhyme nor reason'.

The film enhanced Stewart's standing at MGM, all the same, and on returning to the studio he was kept busy with a series of modest but by no means disgraceful parts. *Wife vs. Secretary* found him supporting Clark Gable and Myrna Loy in a sprightly comedy which also required him to partake in a lengthy kissing scene with a bra-less Jean Harlow ('We did it six times. And that dress … she didn't seem to wear anything under that dress. Well, I forgot my lines. That's what I did'). *Small Town Girl* had him trying out his sincere, unsophisticated country-boy act for the first time on film, and *Speed* allowed him his first starring rôle – as a racing-car test driver – in a wafer-thin B-movie padded out to all of sixty-five minutes with stock footage of speedway events and a tour round a Detroit car factory. It was better, at any rate, than *The Gorgeous Hussy*, a lumpen historical drama in which Joan Crawford starred as

President Jackson's niece, an innkeeper's daughter who is supposed to have had a string of affairs with her uncle's political colleagues. The film doesn't have the courage (or the freedom, under 1930s censorship) to do justice to its own potentially racy scenario, and Stewart looks miserably uncomfortable as one of Crawford's admirers, wandering through the proceedings in top hat and bushy sidewhiskers.

Born to Dance, the seventh of the eight films he was to churn out in 1936, is one of the most interesting from that year. Essentially a vehicle for the engaging, leggy dancer Eleanor Powell, who had recently shot to stardom in *Broadway Melody of 1936* (and here performs a couple of stunning tap numbers), it called for a shy and dignified leading man who could also croon and acquit himself on the dance

His first leading rôle, as the test driver in SPEED (1936).

THE GORGEOUS HUSSY, with Joan Crawford.

BORN TO DANCE: Eleanor Powell

was – Stewart wasn't.

Fronting the chorus line in BORN

TO DANCE.

floor. Cole Porter, composer of the score, thought Stewart might fit the first half of this bill and on 24 April 1936 invited him over to his house to sound out his vocal abilities. 'He sings far from well, although he has some nice notes in his voice' was the verdict, followed by a more enthusiastic 'but he could play the part perfectly'. It was decided to let Stewart have the part, and to dub in another singer for his big romantic number, 'Easy to Love'. When Porter heard Stewart's rendition on screen, however, he felt that it was quite good enough to stay in, and so his is the voice we hear in the finished film.

Although at least one reviewer found his singing and dancing 'painful', Stewart himself looks as though he's having a lot of fun in *Born to Dance*. As petty officer Ted Baker he never gets to wear anything less dapper than naval uniform or white tie and tails, and the rôle allows him to give full vent to his patriotism. (Catching a glimpse of the Statue of Liberty through his periscope in the first scene, his eyes light up with ecstasy as he cries out to the crew members, 'We're home, boys, we're home!') Also, paradoxically, the prevailing froth which characterises most of the movie makes us all the more aware of Stewart's own dramatic alertness, which is clearly well established by now. In the dance routines, while everyone around him is mugging frantically, his facial reactions are just that little bit more naturalistic; as the predatory vamp Virginia Bruce tries to woo him with 'I've Got You under My Skin', he puts on a good show of pleased embarrassment; and even in a tiresome comic interlude with Reginald Gardiner as a policeman conducting an imaginary orchestra, Stewart's eyes are never lazy or off guard, but follow the movements of the baton with amused wonderment.

Further proof of his fast-expanding range was provided by *After the Thin Man*, in which he took the small but crucial part of a jilted lover so racked with jealousy that he turns to murder. While William Powell and Myrna Loy wisecrack their way heartlessly through the detective work, Stewart seems at first to be acting in a different film, playing everything on a note of subdued intensity which is typified by his response to a petulant question from his sweetheart: 'You can't indefinitely go on caring for somebody who doesn't care for you, can you?' 'Well,' Stewart answers slowly, 'it's been done.' The screenplay is taken from a Dashiell Hammett story, and ends with one of those classic everyone-together-in-a-room scenes where the entire cast fires questions and accusations back and forth at one another and nobody in the audience has a clue what's going on. Again it's Stewart who moves things on to a different level, suddenly unmasked as the killer and launching into a barnstorming confession of guilt: 'I killed Robert, but not the way I wanted to. It was too quick, too easy. I wanted to see him suffer like he's made *me* suffer.' At this point we see the first appearance of a mannerism that would recur throughout his career: a quivering hand brought to the mouth and gnawed in a spasm of involuntary anguish (see also, among others, *It's a Wonderful Life, No Highway, Rear Window* and *Vertigo*). Finally he is carried out of the room, kicking, screaming and still wielding his gun. Received wisdom would have us believe that *Winchester '73* (1950) marked the emergence of a new and unprecedentedly violent Stewart persona, but it was prefigured long before he

Nursing his tormented passion for Elissa Landi in AFTER THE THIN MAN; *William Powell looks on.*

teamed up with Anthony Mann and is there for all to see in the closing reel of this otherwise very lightweight film.

As Chico – just your ordinary Parisian sanitary engineer – in Seventh Heaven, *co-starring Simone Simon.*

The year 1936 must have been a draining one for Stewart, but he has always spoken with great fondness of the factory-like system of studio production. 'I've always felt that the studio system is the *ideal* way to make pictures … You worked six days a week. You got there every morning at eight o'clock and you left at six. And if you weren't making a picture – a big part in a small picture, or a small part in a big picture – you were working out in the gym, you were doing tests with other people that they were thinking about signing. You were out on the road with a picture you weren't even in, plugging it from the stage. And there was a *feeling* of sort of … You were a part of something that was *excitement* all the time.' But the downside of this system was an occasionally haphazard approach to casting which might find performers shunted into totally unsuitable rôles; while the actor might learn something from the experience (if only the extent of his own limitations), this was small compensation for any luckless audience who actually sat through the films in question. Better to pass over in near-silence, then, Stewart's performances as Chico, a lovelorn Parisian sewer worker in Henry King's *Seventh Heaven* ('employing for the purpose a remarkably adenoidal Princeton voice', as the *New York Times* noticed), and as Paul North, a moustachioed newspaper reporter in *The Last Gangster*. Little Caesar himself, Edward G. Robinson, was

Leaving his eight-roomed Brentwood home, bought in 1937 after Seventh Heaven *had confirmed his star status.*

borrowed from Warner Brothers to give it some backbone, but MGM were altogether too genteel to do this sort of thing properly, and the film is risibly lacking in the rival studio's characteristic toughness.

Reporters; psychotic murderers; racing-car drivers; crooks on the run; tuneful sailors on shore leave – Stewart had by now certainly proved his versatility. What he had so far crucially failed to establish, however, was a consistent, trustworthy image for audiences to associate with his

Playing the proud sea cadet in NAVY BLUE AND GOLD, with Florence Rice.

name. The first steps in that direction came with his next two movies, which would both feature him as an upright, patriotic young idealist struggling to live up to his own private values in the face of adverse circumstance. *Navy Blue and Gold*, a noxious conflation of the service academy/football film genres, cast him as a midshipman at the Naval Academy in Annapolis – which Stewart himself, of course, had once wanted to attend. The scene where he leaps to his feet to defend the reputation of his dishonourably discharged father won him many admirers (including Frank Capra, as previously mentioned), and Stewart does indeed make the best of a grievously overwritten job; but it seems perverse that so many people should think that this most subtle and diffident of actors is at his best when speechifying. *Of Human Hearts* was slightly better;

On the football field in NAVY BLUE AND GOLD.

An overwrought moment from OF HUMAN HEARTS: Beulah Bondi played his mother, as she was to do in four subsequent films.

here Stewart played the son of a severe minister (Walter Huston), growing up in Ohio just before the Civil War. The plot's manipulative sleights of hand, involving much harrowing self-sacrifice on the part of Stewart's mother in order to send him through medical school, are not very palatable today; nor is the closing sequence in which Stewart returns to his mother and childhood sweetheart, having been lectured on the error of his ungrateful ways by none other than Abe Lincoln himself. But director Clarence Brown's sensitivity to period texture and detail remains impressive, and the film was a brave, uncommercial venture for its time.

The potential humourlessness of the personality that Stewart was beginning to project on screen in these two films was now undercut, just in the nick of time, by *Vivacious Lady*, a well-made George Stevens comedy for which he was loaned out to RKO. He played a young biology professor who falls in love with a night-club singer (Ginger Rogers) and marries her the next day; most of the film is then taken up with comic misunderstandings arising out of his failed attempts to introduce her to his stuffy academic father. Although Stewart doesn't actually appear in the two funniest scenes – a fist-fight between Rogers and her rival, Frances Mercer, and a dance sequence in which his elderly mother, Beulah Bondi, shows an unexpected talent for jiving – he instils much charm into a difficult part, one that requires him to spend a good deal of time rather pointlessly manoeuvring Rogers out of one embarrassing situation and into another. His performance irons out many of the inconsistencies in the character and moulds it smoothly around his own fast-emerging persona, which is neatly defined in one scene where he boasts shyly, 'I've always tried to be a strong man, in a conservative sort of way.'

During and after the making of *Vivacious Lady*, Stewart and Rogers had a brief affair which the actress describes in affectionate but scarcely tremulous terms in her autobiography. Recalling their double dates with Henry Fonda and Lucille Ball, she writes, 'One night, after a hearty meal at Barney's, the boys took us back to their apartment. Everything appeared very romantic, as the lights were turned down low and soft music played in the background. Before Lucy and I knew what had happened, we were danced into the kitchen to wash a week's stack of dirty dishes ... But still, two nicer men you couldn't hope to meet.' Like most of the stories from Stewart's bachelor days, this one casts him in the rôle of wide-eyed innocent rather than aggressive seducer. He

As biology teacher Peter Morgan, blinding Ginger Rogers with science in VIVACIOUS LADY.

Right: Stewart and Ginger Rogers dated for a while after making VIVACIOUS LADY. 'He loved to laugh, and was a smooth dancer,' she recalled.

was also taken in hand, for instance, by Norma Shearer, who insisted on parading her new acquisition about town in a yellow limousine (Stewart slumped low in the back seat in embarrassment) and on giving him a gold cigarette case so that she could ostentatiously ask him for cigarettes at parties. (Stewart, to prove his independence, would fumble in his pocket and hand her a pack of Lucky Strikes.) There are distinct shades of *Sunset Boulevard* in this relationship; and both Fonda and Frank Capra agree that Stewart's strongest romantic appeal at this stage was to women who wanted to 'mother' him.

In a powerfully-written article for *Film Comment*, Kathleen Murphy has argued that we should reject this sexless image of the young Stewart, and cites

Left: *At Simone Simon's birthday party, where Marsha Hunt and William Wyler seem more entertained by his story than Lucille Ball does. The blonde head belongs to Ginger Rogers.*

Below: *Norma Shearer, another conquest from Stewart's bachelor days.*

in particular the moment in *Vivacious Lady* when he seizes the romantic initiative and 'stops Rogers' lips with the blind instinct of a hungry infant – or a turned-on cobra'. It is, perhaps, the tendency to idealise him as the bumbling, guileless, essentially *neutered* country boy that rules out any real possibility of dramatic interest in his next film, *The Shopworn Angel*. This was a remake of a part-silent Gary Cooper movie made in 1929, concerning a naive young soldier stationed at a US army base in New York, who falls for a worldly-wise stage star. The object of Stewart's adoration in this version was played by Margaret Sullavan at her most enchanting. She is in the throes of a rather tired relationship with her cynical manager (Walter Pidgeon), who looks on with lazy amusement at Stewart's cack-handed attempts at courtship. Sullavan and Pidgeon refer repeatedly to Stewart as 'the kid' ('The poor kid doesn't even know he's at the front', 'Nice to know the kid's so happy') and the film does indeed ascribe to him an almost childlike simplicity which sits pretty uneasily on the shoulders of

the thirty-year-old actor. Consequently there are a few scenes – like the attempt to squeeze humour out of his clumsy approach to potato-peeling – that find Stewart doing something he can hardly ever be accused of during the rest of his career: hamming it up. He and Sullavan do salvage one or two good comic-romantic moments, though, most notably their first encounter in the back of a cab, when her icily sarcastic yarn-spinning about the prevalence of cows in New York City ('Yeah, they round them up in Times Square every Thursday afternoon') provides him with an opportunity to register a succession of splendidly-timed double takes.

Young love, Hollywood-style: The Shopworn Angel, with Margaret Sullavan.

Meanwhile, Stewart was about to strike up another screen partnership, one that would have a profound effect on the American public's perception of him from that point onwards. Whether this partnership would serve to enhance or diminish his stature as an actor is a matter of opinion, depending entirely upon the viewer's attitude towards that eminently marketable cinematic commodity that would come to be known as 'Capracorn'.

2

EVERYBODY'S ALL-AMERICAN
1938-1941

Opinions vary as to the merits of Stewart's films with Frank Capra, but what isn't open to doubt is the enormous boost they gave to his career. 'Frank gave me this chance, this tremendous, wonderful rôle, which really started me rolling,' Stewart has said, and it's true that for many of the actor's admirers, the part of Jefferson Smith in *Mr Smith Goes to Washington* constitutes the quintessential Stewart: the upstanding, all-American, small-town boy, loyal to his family, his country, his church and his ideals; the personification of 'rock-ribbed honesty'. Far from being the apex of his career, however, this part was really little more than its starting-point – the clean slate upon which Stewart, in the hands of directors like Hitchcock and Anthony Mann, would later inscribe layer upon layer of more disturbing variation and complexity.

In any case, Capra's favourite hero, the 'little man' standing up for his rights against an army of hostile interests, was already full of inconsistencies by the time Stewart inherited its mantle. The origins of this figure, which came to obsess Capra and to dominate most of his film work from the mid-1930s onwards, can be traced back to a novel published in 1928 under the title *Mr Blue*, by the Irish-American writer Myles Connolly, who subsequently became one of the director's closest friends. Capra seems to have been highly susceptible to the conflicting influences of his stronger-minded associates, and took much of his subsequent 'political' 'thinking' (to use both of these terms loosely) directly from this naive fable about a Christ-like innocent wandering through the modern world spreading sweetness and light wherever he goes. In particular he was impressed by the idea that 'the Lost Cause' is the only one worth fighting for, an idea that would surface with a vengeance in *Mr Smith Goes to Washington*. When Capra first met Connolly at a party in 1930, the writer

The filibuster scene in MR SMITH GOES TO WASHINGTON which some consider one of Stewart's greatest triumphs. He used bichloride of mercury to make his voice go hoarse.

On the set of YOU CAN'T TAKE IT WITH YOU *with Frank Capra – regarded by Stewart as 'a classic example of what a motion picture director should be'.*

took him to task for making films that were 'picture postcards when they could be Sistine Chapels and Mona Lisas', and these remarks sowed the seeds for his future conversion to a more messianic approach to film-making, in which entertainment values would be ruthlessly subsumed to social commentary. That conversion became complete in 1935 when, after a serious illness, Capra claimed to have been visited in hospital by a 'little man' who approached his sick-bed and gave him another dressing-down for making frivolous films for the mass audience: 'The talents you have, Mr Capra, are not your own, *not* self-acquired. God gave you those talents; they are His gifts to you, to use for His purpose. And when you don't *use* the gifts God blessed you with, you are an offense to God – and to humanity.'

How much truth there is in this extraordinary anecdote will always be open to doubt. By the time Capra got his hands on Stewart, anyway, he had kissed goodbye to the carefree comedy of *It Happened One Night* and the low-key eroticism of *The Bitter Tea of General Yen*. The first fruit of his new style had been *Mr Deeds Goes to Town*, in which Gary Cooper played an incorruptible small-town hick who inherits twenty million dollars, and now the director had his sights set on *You Can't Take It with You*, the George S. Kaufman/Moss Hart comedy which had been an enormous hit on Broadway. The play concerned a clash of interests and philosophies between two families – the Vanderhofs, a bunch of freedom-loving eccentrics, and the Kirby family, Wall Street bankers who are desperate to buy up the house in which the Vanderhofs live out their carefree existence. Stewart was given third billing as Tony Kirby, the banker's son who serves to bring the two clans together by falling in love with one of the Vanderhof daughters, played by Jean Arthur.

You Can't Take It with You won the Oscar for Best Picture in 1938, and yet there can be few ordeals more grisly than having to sit through the complete film today. Capra and his long-time screenwriter Robert Riskin broadened out the characterisations disastrously, transforming the Vanderhofs from a charming household of free spirits into a carnival of childish boobies, simpletons whose idea of fun is tinkling away on the xylophone, practising ballet steps around the sitting room or letting off firecrackers in the basement. Despite having no visible means of support (apart from Jean Arthur's work as Stewart's secretary) they manage to employ a team of black servants who luckily do all the washing, cooking and cleaning for them so that they can spend more time amusing themselves with their hobbies. In the film's cringingly embarrassing ending, Grandpa Vanderhof manages to persuade Mr Kirby to give up life on Wall Street and take up the harmonica; we then see them performing 'Polly Wolly Doodle' together while the family cavort ecstatically around them. As Graham Greene observed in his review at the

YOU CAN'T TAKE IT WITH YOU reaches its climax (and not a minute too soon).

The best and most famous scene from You Can't Take It with You: *Stewart and Jean Arthur in the restaurant.*

time, 'This presumably means a crash on Wall Street and the ruin of thousands of small investors, but it is useless trying to analyse the idea behind the Capra films: there *is* no idea that you'd notice.'

With Carole Lombard in Made for Each Other.

Somehow, in the midst of all this nonsense, Stewart managed to salvage three excellent scenes. In his first big courtship scene with Jean Arthur, he's at his most likeable and unaffected, but the breezy amiability of his manner leaves her – and us – in no doubt as to the depth of feeling which lies behind it ('You know, if you scratch around under the surface here, you'll find a proposal lying around'). He's very touching, as well, in the quiet scene (mercifully quiet, compared to the rest of the movie) where he sits her down in the park at night and reminisces about his days as an idealistic college boy, when he studied engineering and had dreams of harnessing solar power, which somehow got forgotten when he arrived on Wall Street. And there is, finally, the justly famous sequence where he takes her to a restaurant and feels a scream coming on – describing its progress from the tips of his feet up through his lungs until the suspense is so great that Arthur can no longer stand it and suddenly starts screaming herself. This sequence is a tribute both to the thoroughness with which Stewart had by now integrated humour into his dramatic range, and to Capra's genuine flair for orchestrating comic situations. Director and actor, in any case, were thunderstruck with mutual admiration by the time the filming was over. Stewart said that he had 'complete confidence in Frank Capra … from the very first day I worked with him. He's a classic example of what a motion-picture director should be. I just hung on every word Frank Capra said.' And the compliment was quickly returned: 'Jimmy Stewart first of all is a very, very fine actor. He can project whatever his thoughts are. He can project what he's dreaming, what's in his heart, what's in his soul. He can let you see that.'

Made for Each Other, which followed immediately after *You Can't Take It with You*, is not the story of Stewart and Capra's new-found love affair but a rather

botched study of marital hardships in which he was paired with the brilliant comedienne Carole Lombard. Lombard was anxious to try out more serious parts, and Stewart was roped in by David O. Selznick to play a weak-willed lawyer who marries her on impulse and subsequently falls out of favour with his boss (to whose daughter he was engaged). Financial difficulties tear the couple apart, but they are reunited in adversity when their baby contracts pneumonia. Until this point the film treads an uneasy line between humour and pathos; a fact confirmed by the preview cards, which showed ambivalent audience reactions and persuaded Selznick to tack on a supposedly nail-biting climax in

Edgar Kennedy, Stewart, Claudette Colbert and Nat Pendleton making heavy weather of It's a Wonderful World.

ICE FOLLIES OF 1939.

which a life-saving serum has to be flown across America through hazards including a snowstorm and a plane crash. In one's memory, unfortunately, this bit of foolishness tends to eclipse the performances of Stewart and Lombard, who were very good together. She was the first of three famous leading ladies with whom he made one-off collaborations that year. The second was Joan Crawford, who had the misfortune to star opposite him in a doomed project called *Ice Follies of 1939*, a musical extravaganza with a Technicolor finale which put severe strain on his skating if not his acting abilities. Crawford's daughter has suggested that her mother was shunted into this film by MGM as punishment for her recent poor record at the box office, but in truth everyone had high hopes for this lavish, big-budget production featuring two of the studio's top players and a spectacular ice show by the Shipstad and Erhardt skaters. The plot was paper-thin, though – insultingly so, when you consider the calibre of these performers – and to anyone who chances upon the movie today it's a mystery why Stewart doesn't look more embarrassed in it.

Finally, there was *It's a Wonderful World*, a none-too-pacy screwball comedy in which he co-starred with Claudette Colbert. The film strained hard to be wacky, casting Stewart wildly against type as a hard-boiled private detective (struggling to bring conviction to lines that would have fallen more easily from the lips of a Bogart or a George Raft, like 'Now get a smile on that kisser of yours or I'll plug you') and requiring him to do a series of uncomfortable impersonations, perhaps the best of which is his turn as a knock-kneed scoutmaster with pebble glasses. The trouble is that this very wackiness had, at this stage in the screwball cycle, become completely formulaic: in films like this, when you see a couple handcuffed together for the night, sending each other to sleep with such endearments as 'You're the most loathsome human being I ever met' and 'The same to you', you know it's only a matter of time before they fall into each other's arms. *It's a Wonderful World* was competently made but there was nothing fresh about it.

Capra posing in the corridor of the MR SMITH set.

Meanwhile, as Colbert and Stewart were swapping their barbed love talk on the MGM sound stages, over at Columbia Frank Capra was busy with the elaborate pre-production for *Mr Smith Goes to Washington*. In Capra's own version of events, it had only taken the first page of a two-page synopsis to convince him that this was a project he simply had to film. 'Before I got to the second page I leaped up, began pacing. Ideas leapfrogged so fast I couldn't keep up with them. "No. Not Gary Cooper and Jean Arthur," I spluttered in short bursts. "No – Jimmy Stewart and Jean Arthur – this is a young senator – Boy Scout leader – naive, idealist."' In fact Capra's memory is at fault. The first press reports in August 1938 announced that Gary Cooper *would* be starring in the film; it was more than five months later that Samuel Goldwyn decided not to lend him out, at which point Stewart was approached instead. But even if he was not the director's first choice, he would for ever afterwards be identified with Jefferson Smith, the bumbling Boy Scout leader who arrives at the US Senate swollen with pride at the thought that he is the chosen representative of his people, only to find that he has been selected as a political stooge by a corrupt pressure group led by Claude Rains and Edward Arnold. Smith and his minders finally come into conflict – as the reader will hardly need to be reminded – over a disputed piece of land which he wants to use for a boys' camp while Rains and co. have plans to turn it into a profit-making development.

Although due caution must be exercised while treading around what is, after all, a cherished piece of Americana, it has to be observed that *Mr Smith Goes to Washington* no longer inspires quite the same uncomplicated enthusiasm with which it was received by many people in its day. It was, without doubt, a tremendous technical achievement: Lionel Banks's set for the Senate chamber was a masterpiece of faithful reproduction, and Capra and his crew members showed enormous resourcefulness in devising the multiple camera set-ups which would keep the climactic action progressing on three different levels (the chamber floor, the rostrum and the press gallery). The film hums with energy and, as always with Capra, a huge team of character actors brings life and authenticity to even the smallest parts. And yet the sermonising verbosity of much of the script constantly goes against the grain of all this surface vitality. Stewart once compared Capra's technique to Hitchcock's, saying that 'although they went about it in different ways, both of them wanted to get the

Arriving with Jean Arthur for work on MR SMITH GOES TO WASHINGTON.

Lionel Banks's set reproduced the US Senate chamber in perfect detail, and was one of the most expensive and elaborate ever built at this time.

story up on the screen visually ... The spoken word was secondary'; yet what could be less cinematic than the climax to *Mr Smith*, which hinges upon the delivery of a twenty-four-hour speech – a speech, moreover, that is required to bear the movie's entire ideological burden, with its endless commonplaces about liberty, 'American ideals' and 'looking out for the other fella'?

Analogous with this tension between verbiage and visual energy is the political confusion at the heart of the film. Capra was astonished that so many journalists and politicians saw it as an attack on the American system, but this might have been anticipated, since although the film revels in quasi-religious shots of Capitol Hill bathed in ecstatic light and close-ups of James Stewart going dewy-eyed as he contemplates the statue of Lincoln, it immediately turns around to tell us that the entire political arena is in fact little more than a playground for cigar-smoking heavies and bully-boys. Here we can see the conflicting impulses of Capra's most influential collaborators coming together to fatal effect, because although the screenplay is nominally the work of Sidney Buchman, a writer of liberal sympathies, there were several important – though uncredited – contributions from Myles Connolly, who was a hardline Catholic and supporter of the far right. Hence the grotesque absurdity of the film's closing sequence, when Claude Rains undergoes a complete political *volte-face* in the space of a few seconds and rushes into the Senate screaming his repentance: a fine actor driven by the inconsistencies of the screenplay to a performance of appalling fakery and amateurism. Buchman himself has always been outspoken on the matter: 'When I watch the film again,' he said, 'I always leave before the end. I detest the suicide of Claude Rains. It was an idiotic idea and I fought against it, without success. All of a sudden you're in a totally unreal situation.'

Buchman insists that the theme of *Mr Smith* is 'that it is necessary to maintain a vigilant attitude even when you think you are living in a democracy', but claims that Capra never understood this. 'His view of the world came down to that of a fairy-tale: at the end the good people had to be rewarded and the evil ones punished ... For him a politician or a capitalist were simply marionettes representing good or evil ... Their meaning didn't exist for him, and I really believe that he never knew what *Mr Smith* actually was saying.' Stewart, too, has always backed off from analysing the thorny political questions which the film itself raises and then does its best to avoid. Once, after

Confronting Claude Rains with his treachery.

proudly reminding an interviewer that 'I was raised in a very definite conservative Republican philosophy', he added, 'I suppose in *Mr Smith* the film could be on the side of the common man and against big business, but to me it was only a matter of right or wrong.' It's one of his favourites among his own films, and he threw himself into the rôle with great enthusiasm. 'He was so serious when he was working in that picture,' Jean Arthur remembered. 'He used to get up at five o'clock in the morning and drive five miles an hour to get himself to the studio. He was so terrified that something was going to happen to him, he wouldn't go any faster.'

It's become routine to acknowledge the final filibuster scene as the highlight of Stewart's pre-war career, and certainly the passion, conviction and sheer stamina that he brings to this sequence aren't open to doubt. But at the same time, it's a one-note performance; a harangue designed to steamroller the viewer into submission. Stewart has to keep pounding away at the audience like this, too, because if we are allowed to pull back for a minute we might remember that all this fuss is about nothing more than the establishment of a 'boys' camp', founded upon the shaky premise that freckle-faced youngsters will be able to learn about 'nature and American ideals' (which apparently go hand in hand). The emotional heat generated by Capra's direction and the haggard sincerity of Stewart's performance camouflage an almost childish simple-mindedness at the heart of Smith's crusade, which scuppers any real possibility of a final confrontation between 'good' and 'evil'. As a piece of *acting*, in fact, Stewart's earlier scene in the Senate is far more affecting, when he makes his maiden speech and rises fumblingly to his feet, his voice shaking with nervous trepidation as he struggles to frame the words. Here the emotions underpinning the situation are real, and the viewer cannot help being won over by the naturalism of Stewart's manner, his oddly gracious awkwardness. The film has not yet started to preach.

What has finally made *Mr Smith* unpalatable to the modern audience, of course, is history. Post-McCarthy, post-Vietnam, post-Watergate, post-Iran-Contra, its insistence on the inevitable triumph of old-fashioned American idealism over political expediency seems less than convincing. When viewing the film today, then, we should perhaps make an effort to see it in its historical context, remembering that back in 1939 its ringing exaltation of America as the land of the free must have carried great symbolic weight, particularly in a

Europe falling under the shadow of fascism. *Mr Smith Goes to Washington* was the film most French audiences voted to see as a 'last request' before the Nazis banned screenings of all American films after the Occupation.

Although Stewart didn't win the Oscar some people thought he deserved for his performance in *Mr Smith*, it nevertheless transformed his standing in Hollywood. From now on he would no longer be regarded simply as another light (if unusually versatile) leading man, but as something much more valuable – an icon: someone who could be invoked as an instantly recognisable emblem of everything that was legal, decent, honest and true about America. It's an image that Stewart re-emphasised in a publicity statement put out at around this time. 'I have my own rules and adhere to them,' he said. 'The rule is simple but inflexible. A James Stewart picture must have two vital ingredients: it will be clean and it will involve the triumph of the underdog over the bully.'

Destry Rides Again, the comedy Western he now made for George Marshall at Universal, qualified on both these counts. In his new-found capacity as Hollywood's Mr Clean, Stewart was called in to act as a 'normalising' presence for Marlene Dietrich, in order to rehabilitate her with the middle-American audiences who had so decisively rejected her at the box office over the last few years. (He would perform a very similar function for Katharine Hepburn in *The Philadelphia Story* a year later.) To this end he was cast as Thomas Jefferson

His first Western rôle, as the tea-drinking cowboy in DESTRY RIDES AGAIN.

Destry – the middle name itself gesturing back towards Capra's film – who is summoned to the unruly town of Bottleneck to act as deputy sheriff. His reputation as a firebrand precedes him, but the townsfolk are amused and delighted to find that he refuses to carry a gun, since he believes that law and order can be imposed without the need to resort to violence. They look forward to a spree of unregulated gambling and pistol-packing, with the occasional pleasant interlude spent listening to sexy *chanteuse* Frenchy (Dietrich), who is a willing accomplice in all this lively amorality. But it seems they have reckoned without Stewart's doggedness and strength of character (he compares himself to a postage stamp which 'sticks to one thing till it gets there') and by the end of the film he has purged the town of its criminal tendencies.

Destry Rides Again is a loud, boisterous and flippant Western, at times reminiscent of *Way Out West*, which is perhaps not so surprising since Marshall had directed a few Laurel and Hardy films earlier in his career. But it also has an interesting sub-text which explicitly connects the more gentle, civilised, non-violent side of Stewart with femininity. It's not just that the women of Bottleneck eventually rally round him and join in a pitched battle with the aggressive menfolk; the film repeatedly makes Stewart himself look feminine. When he first arrives on the stagecoach he is seen carrying a parasol and a canary cage which belong to his travelling companion; at the bar he is offered not hard liquor but first of all 'a nice cup of tea' and then a glass of milk; his avowed intention to 'clean up' the town is turned into a joke by Dietrich when she presents him with a bucket and mop for this purpose; and one female admirer remarks of him, wistfully, 'He's certainly different from the rest of the men you meet out in this country.' The phallic symbolism of the pistol is also made unambiguous – with one of the villains, for instance, referring to the gunless Stewart as 'ladyfingered'. And so it's here, perhaps, that we find a clue to his undoubted appeal for the female audience. Although not lacking in the traditional 'masculine' virtues (Destry does of course know how to use a gun, and will be obliged to do so before the film is over), he doesn't flaunt them or brag about them, and is sensitive to ways in which women might find them threatening or offensive. Stewart could be strong and quiet, gentle and assertive; and he went on to prove it again with his next comedy, Ernst Lubitsch's *The Shop around the Corner*.

Giving Marlene Dietrich (and her career) a leg-up in DESTRY RIDES AGAIN.

On the subject of this film, I might as well declare a personal preference at the outset. It may have been his rôle in *The Philadelphia Story* that won Stewart his only Oscar; it may have been *Mr Smith Goes to Washington* that shot him to stardom; but I believe that *The Shop around the Corner* is by far his best pre-war film, and contains by far his best performance from this period. Or, in the words of Samson Raphaelson, who wrote the film's superb screenplay: 'Stop and contemplate the lanky, drawling young American playing a Hungarian clerk so flawlessly that no one seems to realize it is one of the great performances in cinema history. If you saw the picture ten times, and studied it, you would get a glimmer of the fine sense of detail, the capacity for controlled artistry that resides in Stewart and that Lubitsch delivered to us all.'

The Shop around the Corner, based loosely on a stage play by Nikolaus Laszlo, tells the story of Alfred Kralik (Stewart) and Klara Novak (Margaret Sullavan), two clerks who find themselves perpetually at loggerheads while working for a family-owned leather-goods shop in Budapest. Kralik is meanwhile carrying on an anonymous correspondence with a woman he knows only as 'Dear Friend'; their letters are supposed to concern themselves only with 'cultural subjects', although of course they have been getting gradually more romantic. It cannot remain a secret for long (to the audience, anyway) that Klara herself is the anonymous recipient of these letters, but the film has the intelligence to realise this and makes no great attempt to milk suspense out of the situation. Instead, Raphaelson's screenplay walks the difficult tightrope between comedy and seriousness with astonishing authority, running an ambitious emotional gamut from the tragic suffering of the shop's cuckolded owner, Mr Matuschek (played by Frank Morgan with warmth and dignity), to some broad touches of humour: as, for instance, in a running gag about whether or not the Stewart character is bow-legged which culminates in the film's final shot – a close-up of his calves, with his socks held up by very unglamorous suspenders. It's an image that somehow manages to be at once both absurd and breathtakingly moving and romantic.

This is one of the *quietest* films ever made in Hollywood – the dialogue scarcely rising above a polite whisper, and hardly ever underlined by background music – and the action is almost entirely confined to a single set. The unobtrusiveness of Lubitsch's direction, however, should not mislead us concerning the level of intelligence and commitment with which Raphaelson's conception has been brought to the screen. Although the camera is generally content merely to record the action in medium shot, it will occasionally spring into life and follow the characters' movements with zestful agility: as in the scenes where Kralik strides hopefully towards Mr Matuschek's office, confident of getting his raise, or when Klara scurries to the cloakroom to get her hat and coat on the way to her first date with the unknown correspondent. In both scenes, the camera's sudden mobility invites us to share in the energy of youthful spirits momentarily breaking out from the shackles of their narrow, financially restricted lives. Lubitsch's sympathy for these characters and their milieu is reflected in his own assessment of the movie: 'It is a universal theme

The proprietor of Matuschek and Company watches as Stewart and Margaret Sullavan get acquainted: 'There was a quiet, perceptible, somewhat exclusive intimacy between them on screen.'

and tells a simple story. I have known just such a little shop in Budapest where the film's action takes place ... Never did I make a film in which the atmosphere and the characters were truer than in this film.' His attention to detail can be gauged by his reaction when Margaret Sullavan brought her own costume along to the set – a dress she had picked up for $1.98: 'Too smart for a clerk looking for a job,' Lubitsch decided, and had it altered to be ill-fitting and then left out in the sun until it had a faded appearance.

One sequence in *The Shop around the Corner* bears a superficial resemblance to certain scenes in Frank Capra's *You Can't Take It with You* and *It's a Wonderful Life*. Both of these Capra movies show a hero who thought he was down on his luck being suddenly showered with money by his supportive friends, while Lubitsch's film climaxes with tills ringing merrily and money pouring in on the last shopping day before Christmas at Matuschek and Co. But what makes Capra's scenes feel so hollow is their fundamental inconsistency; all along, these films have been insisting that money doesn't matter and no man is poor while he has his friends, but then when salvation finally arrives, it invariably comes in the form of vast injections of cash. Lubitsch and Raphaelson, though, earn the right to include their sequence because they have been honest enough, throughout the film, to point out that money *does* matter very much, particularly to humble shopkeepers living in straitened circumstances. In fact it's remarkable just how much of the dialogue is preoccupied with wages, bonuses, raises and the cost of living; we are constantly reminded that romantic happiness and financial security are intimately connected, but even this down-to-earth fact is given a beautiful twist in a speech when Kralik attempts to persuade Klara to buy her fiancé a wallet for Christmas: 'A wallet,' he says, 'is not only practical – it's romantic. On one side he carries your last letter. On the other side, your picture. And when he opens it, he finds *you* – and that's all the music he wants.'

Here, as elsewhere in the film, Stewart delivers his lines in a reverent, murmurous undertone. As Pauline Kael has written, it's a performance 'full of grace notes; when you watch later James Stewart films, you may wonder what became of this other deft, sensitive, pre-drawling Stewart'. There can be little doubt that the subtlety and tenderness he brings to the part derive not only from an awareness that he was dealing with superlative material, but from the special undercurrent of feeling between himself and Sullavan. You will never

Making an unexpected rendezvous with Margaret Sullavan in THE SHOP AROUND THE CORNER.

see him look with such rapt adoration at any other actress (although he comes close in his love scenes with Kim Novak in *Vertigo*), and their affection for each other seems to have spilled over on to the set, creating an infectious, light-hearted atmosphere entirely free from the tantrums and personality clashes that traditionally beset other Sullavan films. Lubitsch had only words of praise for his leading lady: 'She's a tonic for the cast ... She'll play pranks on the director, gag with the assistant, conspire with the cameraman or go off riding on the handlebars of Jimmy Stewart's bicycle as though she were a child. Those legends about her feuding with Hollywood seem over.' When Stewart was asked to recall the experience of working with her, the first thing he mentioned was 'Humor. She had great humor. It wasn't mechanical with her. It was a part of her. This was one of the things that made her great. When you'd play a scene with her, you were never quite sure, although she was always letter perfect in her lines, what was going to happen. She had you just a little bit off guard.' Perhaps it was this very sense of being 'a little bit off guard', never quite sure where acting ends and reality (including his own true feelings for the actress) might intrude, that enabled Stewart to give what was undoubtedly his most authentic performance up to that point, in a film that is now gaining increasing recognition (to quote Pauline Kael again) as 'one of the most beautifully acted and paced romantic comedies ever made' and 'as close to perfection as a movie made by mortals is ever likely to be'.

Stewart, Sullavan and Frank Morgan immediately started work on another film together, although in a very different vein. This was *The Mortal Storm*, a moving and imaginative treatment of incipient Nazism and its fracturing of an ordinary German family. The film is credited to Frank Borzage, but a more than usually significant contribution was made by Victor Saville, who had recently arrived at MGM from England. Saville, who was Jewish, produced the movie but asked for his name to be taken off the credits since he didn't want it to be construed as propagandist; he is also

Director Frank Borzage discusses THE MORTAL STORM *with Stewart, Sullavan, Robert Stack and William Orr.*

said to have directed all but a week's worth of the shooting. Even if this is true, *The Mortal Storm* retains all the marks of Borzage's directorial personality, with its unabashed commitment to melodrama, and its sense of characters playing out their small human dramas in the shadow of mighty physical, political and supernatural forces, and above all in its exaltation of Margaret Sullavan, an actress who had already enhanced three of his best films of the thirties.

THE MORTAL STORM: making a stand against the Nazis.

One of the most remarkable things about this movie is the way it picks up on the emotional energy generated by *The Shop around the Corner* and carries it over seamlessly into a completely new context. Thus Frank Morgan's tragic professor, who is made to suffer both for his Jewishness and for his scientific theories which invalidate the Nazi creed, arrives on screen already bearing the authority and lovable crustiness of his Mr Matuschek. Similarly, Borzage capitalises on the intense intimacy which surrounds Stewart and Sullavan by the end of Lubitsch's film, and jeopardises it by putting it under threat from fascist thuggery. The scene where they alone refuse to join in a Nazi sing-along at a beer cellar – standing quietly aloof, united by their instinctive distaste – is a precursor to a very similar sequence in *Cabaret*, but is even more powerful because here we can see that the lovers' feelings for each other are being both brought out into the open and fatally endangered at the same time.

Stewart (improbable though this may sound) plays a young horse-vet living in a village beneath the German Alps; he loves Sullavan but she perversely engages herself to a young student (Robert Young) who has signed up enthusiastically for the Nazi Party. The film climaxes with a chase across the snowswept mountains as Stewart attempts to guide Sullavan to safety across the Austrian border. His quivering grief when she is shot dead just before they reach safety (expressing itself only in numbed repetition of the phrase 'Oh no, Freya, oh no') is as harrowing as anything he ever showed on screen. It was to

Allyn Joslin, Stewart, Rosalind Russell and Clarence Kolb in No Time for Comedy. The audience's reaction was much the same, unfortunately.

be his farewell to Sullavan in more ways than one. This was the last time they acted together, and she would make only five more films before premature deafness blocked her career. She finally admitted herself to a sanatorium and took her own life in 1960.

On loan to Warner Brothers, Stewart now became the victim of a ham-fisted piece of adaptation which attempted to tailor a sophisticated Broadway hit, *No Time for Comedy*, to fit the studio's narrow-minded perception of him. He was required to play Gaylord Esterbrook, a writer of shallow theatrical comedies who is persuaded by a scheming patroness (Genevieve Tobin) to start specialising in more socially-conscious drama. On stage this had been entertaining enough, but bearing in mind that 'the Lubitsch type of light comedy has almost always failed to impress mass audiences', the film's associate producer Robert Lord reluctantly proposed to Hal Wallis that 'as much as I dread the job, I believe that the play should be pretty radically altered –

vulgarized – to make it understandable for a mass audience'. And so Stewart's character was turned unconvincingly into yet another small-town boy on the loose in the big city, and most of the play's good lines were lost. Stewart wanders through the film lazily, unable to get a handle on the material and reduced to a kind of torpor by the constraints of a part he'd already played once too often on film.

In any case, Warners were wrong: he was quite capable of turning his hand to drawing-room comedy, as he proved to everybody's satisfaction when he signed up for *The Philadelphia Story* at MGM. The package for this film had been put together by Katharine Hepburn, who not only commissioned Philip Barry to write the stage play for her, but also managed to retain control of the movie rights. (Her brief affair with Howard Hughes had, at least, won her a powerful financial backer.) Although Spencer Tracy and Clark Gable were her original choices for the parts played by Stewart and Cary Grant, she's unlikely to have been disappointed with her replacements; and George Cukor, her favourite collaborator, was hired to direct.

The Philadelphia Story is a curious film, since, as Andrew Sarris has pointed out, its thinly-veiled subject is actually 'Katharine Hepburn *herself*, and what the American people thought about Katharine Hepburn in 1939, and what Katharine Hepburn realized she had to do in order to keep her career going'. She plays Tracy Lord, a haughty, independent socialite whose first husband (Grant) walked out on her in disgust. (She is frequently referred to as 'virginal', and at one point he calls her a 'married maiden', so we can assume that one of the bones of contention was her refusal to consummate the marriage.) Now she is about to marry a dull but worthy coal tycoon, and although she is determined that the wedding should be shielded from the intrusive gaze of the press ('Who the hell do they think they are, barging in on peaceful people – watching every little mannerism – jotting down notes on how we sit, and stand, and talk, and eat and move?'), it is in fact infiltrated by Macaulay Connor, a reporter from *Spy* magazine, played by Stewart.

It doesn't take much imagination to see here an allegory of Hepburn's own career up to this point: her alleged arrogance, her unpopularity with middle-American audiences, her refusal to play the publicity game, her threatening status as an 'independent' woman. The rather dispiriting programme behind *The Philadelphia Story*, then, is to cut her down to size, bringing out her 'human'

With Katharine Hepburn in THE

PHILADELPHIA STORY.

characteristics and giving her a sharp reminder of good old-fashioned American values; and there was no one better equipped for this task than Stewart, who had only recently given Dietrich a taste of the same medicine in *Destry Rides Again.*

While the film's anti-feminist undercurrent may be objectionable, it would take a particularly humourless ideologue not to enjoy much of *The Philadelphia Story*'s surface brilliance. The screenplay fizzes with wit, Grant underplays his part superbly, and Stewart himself seems to have had no

Acting drunk in THE PHILADELPHIA STORY. *Stewart's hiccups in this scene were accidental, but Grant still managed to react spontaneously, and the take was used.*

trouble rising to the demands of his classy company. His famous drunk scene with Grant was semi-improvised, and you can sense the deliciously edgy rapport between these two great actors in their only screen appearance together. Stewart's love scenes with Hepburn are slightly more forced and mannered: he had to be taken to one side and fed words of encouragement by no less distinguished a visitor than Noël Coward before he could get his tongue around one particularly overwritten passage ('You've got hearth-fires banked down in you, Tracy, hearth-fires and holocausts'). He also insisted on wearing his flannel dressing gown throughout the swimming-pool scenes, claiming, 'If I appear in a bathing suit, I know it's the end of me. I know that and I'm prepared to end my career, but it will also be the end of the motion picture industry.'

He was as surprised as anybody when his performance in this film won him the Academy

Alfred Lunt presents Stewart with the Oscar for Best Actor, February 1941. Stewart gave the statuette to his father, who kept it on display in the window of his hardware store.

Badly miscast as a truck driver in ZIEGFELD GIRL, opposite pouting Lana Turner.

Left: *COME LIVE WITH ME*, with Hedy Lamarr.

Award for Best Actor, and has always regarded this decision as a retrospective tribute to *Mr Smith Goes to Washington*. ('I never thought that much of my work in *The Philadelphia Story*,' he admitted.) Certainly MGM, in the months leading up to this award, gave little sign of realising that they had a valuable property on their hands. He made three very low-key films in rapid succession. *Come Live with Me*, the first and best, was shot between 7 October and 26 November 1940. Stewart plays a writer who marries an Austrian refugee (Hedy Lamarr) so that she can stay in the country, and predictably enough they have fallen in love by the time the film's eighty-five charming, forgettable minutes are up. Then, on 27 November, he started work on *Ziegfeld Girl*, in which he plays a truck driver and, despite his top billing, he is hardly anywhere to be seen in a movie that also stars Lamarr, Lana Turner and Judy Garland. He finished this one on 12 December, and the very next day was on the set of an independent production, *Pot O' Gold*. This was a fairly dire musical comedy with Capraesque social overtones, most notable for one peculiar sequence where Stewart's face appears on the moon and he metamorphoses briefly into a medieval minstrel serenading Paulette Goddard on her balcony.

If there is a sense, in these films, that Stewart was simply going through the motions, the reason is not hard to uncover. War was raging in Europe and he was not happy to stand idly by. He had already been to see the studio chiefs and told them that he intended to enlist as soon as possible: this presumably explained why they were happy to fritter him away in such indifferent vehicles. In the meantime, for Stewart, it was merely a question of waiting until the call came.

Pictured just before he signed up for the US Air Force.

3

TOUGHEN IT UP
1941-1950

To describe Stewart as willing to go to war against Germany would be an understatement: desperate is nearer the mark. Although he was technically exempt on the grounds of age, he had no intention – just like his father and grandfather before him – of letting the action pass him by. Legend has it that when the army initially rejected him as underweight, he reapplied and managed to put on the extra pounds by denying himself bowel and bladder movements for thirty-six hours prior to the medical. This gives us some idea of the extent of his determination.

Stewart would serve in the army for roughly four and a half years: half of that time spent training in America, and half of it engaged in bombing missions from English air bases. On 22 March 1941, he enlisted as Private James Maitland Stewart 0433210. As an experienced pilot, he was drafted into the Air Corps: for this purpose he had recently been clocking up as many air miles as he could in his own civilian plane, a three-passenger Stinson HW75 (in which he used to fly home from Hollywood every Christmas). By July Stewart had been promoted to Corporal, and by December to Second Lieutenant. Taking time out only to attend the 1942 Oscar ceremony – where he presented an award to Gary Cooper – and to take part in a radio version of *The Philadelphia*

Back to Hollywood for the 1942 Oscar ceremony, accompanied by Ginger Rogers.

March 1941: Stewart is sworn in to the US Army.

Story with Cary Grant and Katharine Hepburn, he proceeded through advanced flight school and received more than a hundred hours of training in New Mexico. By now a fully-qualified B-17 pilot, he was sent to Gowan Field, Idaho, to spend nine months as a flying instructor and squadron officer. The call to action finally came in August 1943. Stewart was posted to Tibenham air base in Norfolk, and England became his home for the next two years.

Here he was promoted to Major, and served as Group Operations Officer for the 453rd Bombardment Group. The promotion was overdue, but Stewart had been refusing it 'until my junior officers get promoted from lieutenants'. He was now in command of more than fifty Liberator bombers and led twenty raids over German cities including Berlin, Bremen and Brunswick. For his part in the latter raid, which was particularly hazardous, Stewart was awarded the Distinguished Flying Cross and the Croix de Guerre. 'Those missions were no joke,' he has said, 'especially early on when we had no fighter support and were flying daytime raids. There was always so much flak, and we'd get hit. I remember once we lost two engines: but somehow we always made it home.'

Further promotion followed: he became a Colonel in April 1945 and was appointed Chief of Staff for the Second Combat Wing of the Eighth Air Force. His nights were spent at a desk plotting missions, while the days were passed

waiting anxiously at the base for the return of the planes whose safety depended upon his foresight and organisational skills. According to some of his colleagues, it was at this time that Stewart's hair acquired the sheen of grey that would show up so distinctively in his Technicolor films of the 1950s.

Almost fifty years later, he would tell an interviewer that his military experience was 'something that I think about almost every day: one of the great experiences of my life'. In response to the question 'Greater than being in the movies?', he answered unhesitatingly, 'Much greater.' He had been the first film star to enlist and the first to fly in combat. By the time of his return home to America in September 1945, he was Commander of the

1944: Stewart lends a hand at the opening of a new Aero Club 'somewhere in England', where the first cup of coffee is being served by Brigadier General Edward J. Timberlake.

Giving a press conference at the Savoy Hotel in London, December 1943.

As Group Operations Officer for
the 453rd Bombardment Group,
Stewart confers with members of
a bomber crew about to take off
on a combat mission over
German-occupied Europe.

27 August 1945: Colonel James
Stewart travels home from
England, along with 16,000
other American soldiers, on
board the Queen Elizabeth.

Stewart receives the Croix de
Guerre during a ceremony
honouring numerous US Eighth
Air Force men for 'exceptional
services' in connection with the
liberation of France.

Reunited the next day wit

mother and father, at the .

Regis Hotel, New York.

Second Combat Wing, and over the next twenty years he would retain close links with the American military establishment, finally retiring from the Air Force Reserve in 1968 as a Brigadier General.

Stewart did not have to wait long to get back into the movies. In his own words, 'I'd decided some time before coming back to Hollywood that if I could, I'd make my first picture with Capra. Looking back over the pictures I'd done before going away, I felt that the two previous ones I'd made under his direction had been, to me at least, the most satisfying.' And so on 5 November 1945 he signed up with Liberty Films – the new independent company formed by Capra, William Wyler, George Stevens and Samuel Briskin – to star in *It's a Wonderful Life.* This time Stewart was the first actor to be considered for the rôle of George Bailey, the pivotal figure in a project with its origins in a story called *The Greatest Gift* by the writer Philip Van Doren Stern. Stern had printed it privately and circulated it to his friends as a Christmas card in 1939. Rights to the story had been bought by RKO, but three successive screenwriters had failed to wrest a usable treatment out of this brief, quirky parable, which concerned a would-be suicide who gets a unique chance to see what the world would have been like if he had never lived. When Capra was first shown the story by RKO studio chief Charles Koerner, he had (again, if his own account of events is to be believed) another of his instantaneous reactions: 'It was the story I had been looking for all my life! Small town. A man. A good man, ambitious. But so busy helping others, life seems to pass him by. Despondent. He wishes he'd never been born. He gets his wish. Through the eyes of a guardian angel he sees the world as it would have been had he not been born. Wow! What an idea.'

Capra met up with Stewart on 10 October 1945 to pitch the story to him. It was the first time they had seen each other for several years, and the reunion did not go particularly smoothly. Capra thought that the actor looked 'bored' as he outlined the film to him, and even as he told it, 'The story evaporated into thin air, flew out the window.' However, Stewart had already offered to do the movie sight unseen, and didn't seem to be at all concerned by the elusiveness of the plot. There were reasons, in fact, why a story about a hero who feels 'despondent' might have exerted a strong personal appeal to him at this time, since he was profoundly shaken by his wartime experiences, which had caused him to doubt both his faith and the fundamental worth of his chosen career. A devout Presbyterian all his life, for a brief period after the war he stopped going to church altogether. It took parental intervention to sort the problem out. 'My father came on a visit while I was living in Brentwood,' Stewart recalled, 'and around nine o'clock on Sunday morning he asked, "Where do you go to church around here?" And I said, "Well, I don't think there is a Presbyterian church around here. Since the

His first post-war trip home. Stewart's mother is flanked by his sisters Mary (left) and Virginia (right). His father Alex was a powerful influence who was angered, at around this time, to find that Stewart had given up going to church.

Stewart's troubled American hero sinks into suicidal despair in IT'S A WONDERFUL LIFE. Capra's remedy was to provide him with a crinkle-faced guardian angel (Henry Travers).

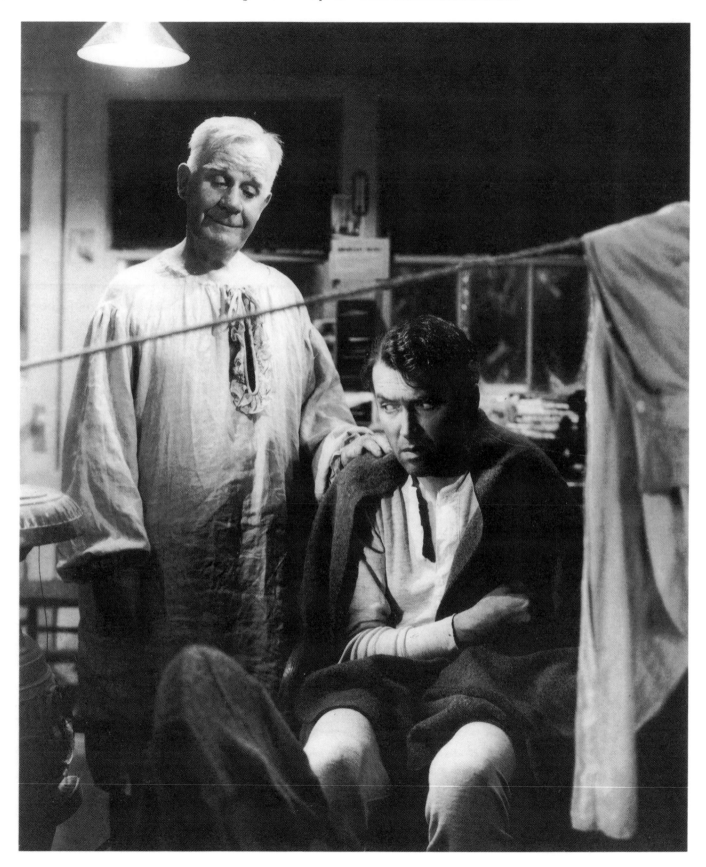

war I just haven't …" He didn't like that, so he said, "I think I'll take a walk," and about three quarters of an hour later he came back with four men I'd never seen before and said, "I'd like you to meet so-and-so and so-and-so – they're elders of the Presbyterian church which is just three blocks from here."' The upshot was that Stewart resumed his attendance at services, and even helped to finance the building of a new church a few years later.

As for his doubts about the usefulness of his career, these repeatedly surfaced on the set of *It's a Wonderful Life* until a quiet word from Lionel Barrymore (who was playing the film's villain, Henry Potter) helped him to see the light. Stewart was apparently agonising over the question of whether acting was not only worthwhile but even 'decent', when Barrymore picked him up indignantly on this word and asked – according to Capra – 'if he thought it was more "decent" to drop bombs on people than to bring rays of sunshine into their lives with his acting talent'. This argument appeared to hit home, and Stewart was further reassured when it soon became obvious that he'd lost none of his ability in his four and half years away from the movies. 'After a week or so of working I just knew that it was going to be all right … I hadn't lost it. *This* was what had kept me awake nights.'

Stewart's soul-searching apart, the atmosphere on the set was buoyant and harmonious. Capra himself has said that he was plagued by 'a loneliness that was laced by the fear of failure' when he started shooting the picture (it was his first film away from a major studio, and all the pre-war collaborators upon whom he had depended so heavily were, for one reason or another, unavailable for this one). But the rest of the cast and crew were spurred on by his boundless energy and their enthusiasm for the material, which would occasionally cause them to overlook some of the potential difficulties: it's not very appropriate, for instance, that the new, mature, grey-haired Stewart should have had to spend most of the early scenes in his first post-war film impersonating a gangly high-school student, and yet he has admitted, 'As a matter of fact, I was having so much fun on the film that it didn't bother me at all. It never occurred to me.'

It's a Wonderful Life opened to reasonable but not outstanding business, was completely eclipsed at the Oscars by Wyler's *The Best Years of Our Lives* (which caught the post-war mood more accurately) and received mixed notices: many reviewers liked it but the British and East Coast critics were occasionally savage,

Stewart and Ellen Ross arrive at the Oscars with Capra and his wife. Their smiles would not survive the evening.

calling it 'a figment of simple Pollyanna platitudes', 'an orgy of sweetness' and 'an embarrassment to both flesh and spirit'. Over the last twenty years, however, the film has been elevated to a realm above and beyond the reach of criticism, becoming a key element in America's Yuletide ritual through frequent television screenings. Even hard-boiled Humphrey Bogart is said to have shown it (tears streaming down his face) to his family and friends every Christmas Day, and sophisticated New Yorkers throw annual parties for the specific purpose of watching

Stewart (aged nearly forty) playing George Bailey (aged nearly twenty). As Henry Fonda once said, 'When Jim stops pretending to be young, he'll become a great artist.'

it in the congenial company of other tearful devotees. On top of which it is, of course, James Stewart's firm favourite among his own movies. For most people it seems that the film's conviction and emotional momentum – to say nothing of Stewart's astonishing performance – carry all before them. And yet there are several evasions and contradictions at its heart. Most notably, the depiction of 'Pottersville' – the nightmarish vision of how quaint little Bedford Falls would have turned out if George Bailey hadn't been there to save it – looks feeble today: the worst the film can come up with to replace Bedford Falls's 'pleasant little middle-class sections' (to quote from the published screenplay) is an exaggeratedly *noir*ish world of gin palaces, tough-faced hookers, seedy boarding houses, frustrated old maids and even the odd jazz club (which would at least provide employment, presumably, for some of the black people who in Capra's 'pleasant … middle-class' version of things are conspicuous by their absence). Besides, if Bailey *alone* has prevented this from coming to pass, isn't this a damning comment on the lack of enterprise and resilience among all the other 'little men' who live in Bedford Falls? And if small-town life is so great, why can it only be saved, in the end, by a large cash donation from the one friend of Bailey's who has managed to *leave* his home town and make a name for himself in business?

For those viewers of the film (a minority, it seems) who are troubled by such questions, its climactic scenes – where the screen is awash with tearful smiles,

IWL-89

All's well that ends well: Bailey's buddies rally round.

pealing bells and banknotes falling like snowflakes – can only be a hollow embarrassment. *It's a Wonderful Life* does succeed on another level, though: as a deeply uncomfortable portrayal of the compromises and neuroses that lie at the heart of American family values. At his worst moments of despair, the violence shown by Stewart towards his terrified family is real and harrowing, and the perpetual frustration of his attempts to escape the strait-jacket of Bedford Falls makes the film almost as surreal and claustrophobic as Buñuel's *The Exterminating Angel* (where a group of well-heeled guests find that their

Right: With co-star Donna Reed in a publicity shot for IT'S A WONDERFUL LIFE.

repeated attempts to leave a dinner party are inexplicably thwarted). Take away its implausible resolution and sugar-coating of supernatural whimsy, and *It's a Wonderful Life* offers a vision of small-town life as explicitly disturbing as anything in the work of David Lynch. In this respect it marks the true beginning of the darker, more troubled side of Stewart's persona which would become increasingly visible over the next decade.

The stars of MAGIC TOWN in a studio portrait.

Capra's film was still in post-production when Stewart began work on *Magic Town*, which had a very similar setting and was written and produced by one of Capra's former colleagues, Robert Riskin. It's been suggested that Riskin directed most of it as well, with the credited director, William Wellmann, only coming in to finish off the last week, but Wellmann himself has bravely shouldered responsibility for the film: 'I was in on that thing from the beginning, and I wish I never started it. It stunk! It's not my kind of film.' The story's unlikely premise was that Stewart, playing an opinion pollster, discovers a 'magic town' called Grandview where the opinions of the people exactly reflect those of the United States as a whole. He moves in, posing as an insurance salesman, and gradually rises to become a respected figure in the community, all the while conducting the clandestine polls with which he hopes to make his fortune. The thrust of the movie is to educate Stewart, cast against type for once as a go-getting New Yorker, into the simple values of small-town life – with some romantic assistance, naturally enough, from a saintly

With Jane Wyman in MAGIC TOWN.

schoolteacher played by Jane Wyman. But comparison with a recent Bill Murray/Andie MacDowell picture, *Groundhog Day*, which also traced a city slicker's conversion to homely values, only shows up the earlier film's inadequacies. *Magic Town* has a good sprinkling of funny moments (notably a scene where Stewart and Wyman try to shout each other down by reciting poetry, with his version *The Charge of the Light Brigade* getting the better of her

*Long-time friends Stewart,
Fonda and Burgess Meredith
enjoy an old boys' reunion in ON
OUR MERRY WAY.*

Hiawatha), but it finally loses its way with an irredeemably dreary sub-plot about the citizens' attempts to raise money for a new civic centre. It also suffers from the fact that Stewart's moral conversion takes place almost invisibly; rarely convincing in parts that require him to act cynical, he already looks like the archetypal home-town boy when the film begins, whereas Murray's transformation from meanness to folksy do-goodery in *Groundhog Day* takes the audience on a convincing and surprising journey.

Time magazine drew attention to the slight sense of *déja vu* which weakens the film, by describing it as 'another of those serio-comic fables in favour of the American way of life which it appears cannot be made without James Stewart'. Stewart himself remembers another review (or perhaps an exaggerated version of the same one) which began: 'If we have to sit through another picture while that beanpole stumbles around, taking for ever to get things out ...' These were not the sort of remarks calculated to make a battle-weary war veteran feel welcome back in Hollywood. One brief respite from his problems was provided when he and Henry Fonda teamed up to play two struggling jazz musicians in a sprightly episode (directed by John Huston and George Stevens) at the beginning of an all-star compilation movie called *On Our Merry Way*; but it was let down by the weakness of the other stories, and the film made little impact. And so, realising that 'I wasn't going across any more', and 'no one was going to see the two pictures I had made when I returned to civilian life', Stewart tried a swift change of tactic and returned to the stage for the first time in twelve years.

The chosen vehicle was *Harvey*, Mary Chase's immensely popular comedy about a gentle alcoholic who imagines that he is being accompanied everywhere by a giant white rabbit. Conceived as a piece of cheerful escapism for wartime audiences, it had already been running on Broadway for three years when Stewart stepped into the part left vacant by veteran actor Frank Fay. Although at first overshadowed by memories of his well-loved predecessor (who at least had the appearance of a wizened alcoholic, whereas Stewart, as one critic observed, 'just doesn't look like the kind of man who ever spent much time in a bar-room'), he subsequently made the part of Elwood P. Dowd very much his own, and would reprise it later in his career on both stage and television.

Universal's film version of *Harvey*, made in 1950, is a faithful adaptation of the stage play, written with Mary Chase's collaboration. Although lacking in most of the cinematic virtues, it does preserve a valuable record of Stewart's performance, which is one of his best. We are back here to the subtle, *sotto voce* Stewart of *The Shop around the Corner*, and the screenplay indulges him with a generous succession of long, richly textured speeches, full of memorable lines and forever going off at unexpected little tangents. Sensing that his function is to provide a still, quiet centre at the heart of much frenetic comic activity, Stewart luxuriates in these opportunities and his delivery rarely accelerates beyond what Josh Logan once referred to as a 'stately pavane'. This, for instance, is how he describes the reaction of strangers to the experience of meeting Harvey for the first time:

> They come over. They sit with us. They drink with us. They talk to us. They tell us about the great big terrible things they've done and the great big wonderful things they're going to do. Their hopes, their regrets. Their loves, their hates. All very large, because nobody ever brings anything small into a bar. Then I introduce them to Harvey, and he's bigger and grander than anything they can offer me. When they leave, they leave impressed.

Beneath its unassuming surface, there was also something genuinely subversive going on in *Harvey*. It refuses to condemn Dowd's alcoholism (although peculiarly enough the Hollywood Production Code would not allow him to be shown drinking in the film – only ordering drinks for others) and it challenges easy distinctions between sanity and insanity, reality and hallucination, insisting upon the qualitative superiority of Dowd's life even though it is lived out in an alcoholic haze and in the company of 'a lot of riff-raff – people you never heard of before'. Before laying too much stress on Stewart's conservatism, then, we should remember the lifelong affinity he showed with this part. He was so thoroughly in sympathy with the whole conception, in fact, that the film's director Henry Koster found working with him to be 'without any doubt one of the most pleasant experiences of my life'. Asked to elaborate, he said, 'It must have been his spirit. There was very little friction, ever, only ambition and craftsmanship and precision, just doing it right professionally. On top of that he put the whipped cream of great talent. That's the best way I can

Josephine Hull and Cecil Kellaway confront the dreaded portrait in Henry Koster's film version of HARVEY.

express it. Not that he was overbearing. It was just his goodness and his talents. He was always the first on the set. He knew all his dialogue, every scene. He made suggestions that were never out of place or out of character.'

It wasn't always like that, because on stage in the summer of 1947 Stewart got some of the worst reviews of his career for his performance in *Harvey* – even if the police did have to be called in to control the crowds outside the theatre. It seemed there was nothing he could do, at this point, to convince the press that he was back on course. A reporter sent by the *New York Times* to do an interview with him cheerfully admitted that the title of the piece had already been decided upon: *The Rise and Fall of Jimmy Stewart.* 'I realised I'd better do *something,*' Stewart said. 'I couldn't just go on hemming and hawing – which I sometimes overdid, too. I looked at an old picture of mine, *Born to Dance.* I wanted to vomit! I had to … toughen it up.'

His first attempt to 'toughen it up' came with *Call Northside 777*, a dour true-life crime story made by Henry Hathaway at Twentieth Century-Fox. (On the advice of his agent, Stewart had by now gone freelance.) He played P.J. McNeal, a reporter on the *Chicago Times*, who gets drawn reluctantly into the investigation of an alleged miscarriage of justice. As in this director's earlier film, *The House on 92nd Street,* much use was made of voice-over commentary and location shooting to provide a veneer of authenticity. The story is absorbing enough, but there's not much to do with a movie like this except to admire the attention to detail – an area in which Stewart, as usual, scores highly. He makes a convincing reporter (his proficiency at the typewriter certainly looks real enough) and although his most naturalistic acting comes in the low-key scenes of domestic contentment with his wife (Helen Walker), he makes a serious effort to sound abrasive and strident when haranguing

With Lee J. Cobb in CALL NORTHSIDE 777.

the wrongly accused 'murderer' in prison. The film itself is no masterpiece, but here we are beginning to see the tentative emergence of a new Stewart: his manner more aggressive, his voice louder (perhaps from all those years of having to shout his commands over the drone of aircraft engines); and in the scene where he spends a sleepless night with his wife, conscience-stricken over the article he has just penned, he comes one step closer to the tormented characterisations of the Mann and Hitchcock films.

CALL NORTHSIDE 777: dingy realism and low-life characters.

In fact, Stewart and Hitchcock were now about to collaborate for the first time. The director was preparing to fulfil a ten-year ambition by making a film of Patrick Hamilton's stage success *Rope*, and was looking for someone to play the crucial rôle of Rupert Cadell, a college lecturer whose abstract philosophical ideas about the expendability of human life inspire two of his students to commit a real murder for the thrill of it. Cary Grant was the first choice, but RKO were not in the mood for lending him out; Stewart was approached next, and after negotiating a threefold increase in his fee he agreed to do it, whereupon he found himself caught up in an extraordinary technical experiment. Wishing to preserve the rigorous time scheme of Hamilton's play – in which, according to the stage directions, 'The action … is continuous, and the fall of the curtain at the end of each Act denotes the lapse of no time whatsoever' – Hitchcock decided to shoot the film in long, continuous takes, each lasting ten minutes, without a single cut.

The difficulties imposed upon the cast by this method were considerable. If, eight or nine minutes into the take, they fluffed their lines or bumped into a table on the single, confined set, the whole take would have to be started again from the beginning. As Hitchcock has proudly explained, 'Every movement of the camera and the actors was worked out first in sessions with a blackboard … Even the floor was marked and plotted with numbered circles for the twenty-five to thirty camera moves in each ten-minute reel. Whole walls of the apartment had to slide away to allow the camera to follow the actors through narrow doors, then swing back noiselessly to show a solid room. Even the furniture was "wild". Tables and chairs had to be pulled away by prop men, then set in place again by the time the camera returned to its original position, since the camera was on a special crane, not on tracks, and designed to roll through everything like a juggernaut.'

To compound these problems, the perpetual motion of the set and the camera made too much noise, so that it became impossible to record the dialogue properly. Hitchcock's solution, according to Stewart, was bizarre: 'Instead of shooting it all and having us loop the dialogue afterwards, he did something I've never seen done before or since. He'd do one take for the camera, but with no microphones. Then he took all the cameras away and had about ten moving microphones on booms, and we'd then do the same scene following the same moves, for sound only. No walls were moved. It was amazing that the soundtrack in all but about five or six places, where it had to be redubbed, fitted perfectly. The fact that we were doing it with all the mechanical things happening meant that we got so practised in our lines that it became automatic to give the same reading.'

In such circumstances it would be surprising if some of this 'automatic' quality did not seep into the performances, and indeed Stewart – along with his fellow-actors – looks wary and subdued throughout the film. On top of which, his character is wretchedly conceived: in Hamilton's play he's a hyper-intelligent cynic who can see no real distinction between war and mass murder. (Needless to say this analogy did not survive into the movie.) But Hitchcock, who liked the idea of casting Stewart because 'he's not an uneducated oaf, you

Cast and director of ROPE.

Stewart watches a game with Monty Stratton himself, who served as technical adviser on the film about his own life.

can believe him as a professor, doctor, family man', turned Rupert Cadell into an altogether more lightweight figure, who affects to regard murder as little more than a black joke ('Why, think of the problems it can solve: unemployment, poverty, standing in line for theatre tickets ...'). Consequently the film never has any real intellectual grounding, and flounders way out of its depth when it starts going on about 'the lives of inferior beings' and 'traditional moral concepts of good and evil'.

At one point during the shooting, Stewart claims that he went to Hitchcock and said, '"You're really missing out on a wonderful opportunity here. You ought to build bleachers [tiered planks forming a seating stand] around the set and charge them five bucks to come in" – because the movement of the camera and the walls and everything was much more interesting than what we were saying.' This is actually a very perceptive remark, because it's painfully clear that all of Hitchcock's energies on *Rope* were directed towards technical experiment at the expense of drama; even the music on the soundtrack, François Poulenc's *Mouvement Perpétuel No. 1*, was chosen not to underscore any emotional content but simply as a knowing reference to the camera's restless activity. *Rope* may exert a certain buffish fascination on a first viewing, but otherwise it's an arid and monotonous film, and an inauspicious foretaste of what was later to become one of Stewart's most important professional associations. At the box office, it did nothing to break his post-war run of bad luck.

Right: THE STRATTON STORY.

That run came to an end not with *You Gotta Stay Happy*, a misconceived, would-be zany comedy co-starring Joan Fontaine, but with *The Stratton Story*, which found Stewart working back at his old studio, MGM. It was the first of three biopics in which he would portray great American heroes – in this case Monty Stratton, the big-league pitcher with the White Sox whose baseball career was halted when he lost part of his leg in a hunting accident. The film shows Stratton lapsing into depression and self-pity until he sees his baby son taking his first tentative steps: this inspires him to strap on an artificial limb and start walking again. Finally he makes his comeback on the baseball field. Although this sort of stuff can hardly cut much ice with modern audiences, it's not as bad as it sounds, and the combination of Stewart's pained idealism with the toothy cheerfulness of June Allyson, who played his eternally supportive wife (as she did in *The Glenn Miller Story* and *Strategic Air Command*) proved extremely popular: *The Stratton Story* was Variety's sixth-highest-grossing movie of 1949. Once again, however much you resist the thread of sentimentality that runs through the film, it's hard not to be impressed by the thoroughness – almost De Niro-like, one might say – with which Stewart immerses himself in the part. He was cast at Stratton's own request, and was 'determined to get as much instruction as possible … so I'd look right pitching a ball. Two months before the picture started, Monty Stratton came up. Every day, for three hours, back in the backlot of MGM, I just threw the ball. And Monty kept after me and after me. He'd say, "You're not using your wrist at the right time." It paid off. I got a lot of reaction. Instead of fan letters, I got baseballs to sign.'

Stewart followed *The Stratton Story* with *Malaya*, which he admits was a 'real potboiler'. He played a wartime journalist who agrees to take part in a perilous scheme to smuggle rubber away from the Japanese, and it was one of the few times he allowed himself to co-operate with Hollywood's mythologising of World War II. Undertaken largely for the pleasure of working with Spencer Tracy (who was 'more cantankerous than usual' during the making of the film), it is one of his least interesting movies from any period. *Broken Arrow*, on the other hand, highlights the intriguing contradiction between Stewart's intransigent political views and his willingness to experiment as an actor. This Delmer Daves film, made at Twentieth Century-Fox, took him back to the Western for the first time since *Destry Rides Again* and also brought him a long

Even Stewart, Spencer Tracy and Sidney Greenstreet could breathe little life into MALAYA.

way from the rigidly conservative ethos that had surrounded the making of *The Stratton Story*. There he had been directed by Sam Wood, a hawkish conservative and president of the notorious Motion Picture Alliance for the Preservation of American Ideals; now he was taking on a film of markedly liberal tendency which had originally been a project of Joseph Losey's, with a screenplay by Albert Matz which, for political reasons (Matz was one of the Hollywood Ten who had been imprisoned for refusing to co-operate with the

Riding into the heart of potential danger in BROKEN ARROW.

House Un-American Activities Committee), had to be credited to Michael
Blankfort, another liberal writer who was himself later blacklisted.

Broken Arrow was an early manifestation of liberal guilt about the treatment
of native Americans at the hands of Hollywood and, for that matter, America
itself. In it Stewart plays Tom Jeffords, a Civil War veteran now prospecting for
gold in Arizona. The year is 1870, and Jeffords, sickened by the oppression
visited upon the Apaches and the endless cycle of killing that has ensued, takes

*Making his peace with Jeff
Chandler – Hollywood's idea of
an 'authentic' Apache chieftain.*

it upon himself to act as intermediary between the two sides, and to this end sets about learning the Apache language and customs. Unfortunately most of the customs portrayed in the movie – such as the 'blood ceremony' between Stewart and his Apache bride, Debra Paget – are pure invention on the part of the film-makers. Furthermore, the film did not have the courage to use any native Americans in its cast and so the Apache chief has to be played by Jeff Chandler – who appears, in the words of *New York Times* critic Bosley Crowther, 'twice as clean and stalwart-looking as James Stewart ... Mr Chandler carries himself with the magnificence of a decathlon champion at the Olympic Games and speaks with the round and studied phrasing of the salutatorian of a graduating class.'

Instead of being genuinely tolerant of racial difference, then, the film pretends that it doesn't exist: beneath their red skins, it seems, these people are simply honest-to-goodness all-Americans, just like the rest of us. (Stewart expresses his pleased surprise at one point on discovering that 'Apache men had a sense of fair play'.) It's a film full of essentially good intentions which those involved apparently have no idea how to put into practice. *Broken Arrow* sparked off a good deal of debate at the time and was extremely popular – much more so than Anthony Mann's *Devil's Doorway*, made at the same time, which tackled a similar theme more dourly (and perhaps with greater integrity). It also started a brief fashion for socially-conscious Westerns, but whether it managed to change anyone's attitude to native Americans is doubtful. Forty years later, after all, it had been forgotten to the extent that Kevin Costner's *Dances with Wolves* could cover identical ground and yet still be heralded by some as a breakthrough in racial awareness. Like the Costner movie, *Broken Arrow* relied upon a popular, trustworthy American hero to sugar the pill of its liberal message. Whatever the film's limitations, it is to Stewart's credit, at least, that he was keen to take on this function at a time when most of his fellow-conservatives were busy naming names to the industry's witch-hunters.

Shortly after returning from the Arizona location he married Gloria Hatrick McLean, a wealthy, divorced ex-model and socialite some ten years his junior. They had met at a dinner party given by Gary Cooper, and the

Out on a date with the ex-model Gloria McLean at Ciro's, a Hollywood night club, in September 1948. A year later they would be married.

ceremony (which took place on 9 August 1949, in the Brentwood Presbyterian Church which Stewart himself had helped to fund) marked the beginning of a happy, monogamous partnership which to date has lasted even longer than his forty-one years of bachelorhood. His new wife already had two young sons from her previous marriage, but Stewart eased himself into the rôle of father with grace and good humour: 'When I arrived, the children looked on me as a kind of boarder. It could have been difficult, but I just approached this situation quietly. I took it easy. They saw that I paid my rent regularly, didn't come in too late at night, and was on quite good terms with the manageress. On our honeymoon in Honolulu Gloria phoned them up and asked them if they wanted to speak to Father. "Who?" they asked.' Two years later he became a father in his own right when Gloria gave birth to twin daughters.

No whiff of scandal or domestic crisis has ever hung around the marriage. 'I can honestly say that in all the years we've been married, Jimmy never once gave me cause for anxiety or jealousy,' his wife has said. 'The more glamorous the leading lady he was starring opposite, the more attentive he'd be to me. He knew the insecurities I was going through, and made quite sure that they were totally unfounded. His consideration was incredible and one of the reasons why our marriage has lasted so long and is still so good.'

4

MANN'S STEWART: 'A LITTLE ON THE CRAZY SIDE' 1950-1955

Careers happen by accident. This is a hard lesson for the film actor to learn, and a particularly hard one in the case of Stewart. He had an intelligent and objective approach when it came to making career choices, but in spite of this the results were sometimes disappointing. His decision that Capra should direct his first post-war film, for instance, had looked perfectly sensible on paper, and yet *It's a Wonderful Life* did nothing to instigate a comeback. His experience on the film version of *Harvey* provided a particularly extreme reminder that the importance of the chance factor should never be underestimated. Stewart lobbied hard to get the part, was extremely good in it, and the film flopped; but tied in with his package at Universal was another movie – a project that had been knocking around the studio for some time, to no great effect – which would indirectly provide him with permanent financial

Welcoming his new wife to the set of WINCHESTER *'73.*

security as well as opening up a whole new untapped seam of dramatic potential. This movie was *Winchester '73.*

As a bearded con in CARBINE WILLIAMS – *perhaps his least-remembered film of the fifties.*

It had originally been Fritz Lang's idea to make a historical film about the development of the Winchester rifle, but he abandoned it after a couple of years, and when Borden Chase came to write the final screenplay all the earlier drafts were jettisoned. When the script was nearly finished, Chase was approached by the producer Aaron Rosenberg who asked him what he thought of the idea of casting James Stewart in the lead.

He was shocked at first (this was before anyone had seen *Broken Arrow*, which had been held back by Fox for more than a year) but then thought, 'Wait a minute. He was in the Air Force, he knows how to kill … You know, when you command a wing of fighters in a war, you're not exactly soft.' So Stewart was offered the part, and all they needed now was a director. Rosenberg suggested Anthony Mann, having been impressed by *Border Incident*, his thriller about illegal immigration on the Mexican border, and Stewart concurred: he had admired Mann's recent Western *Devil's Doorway* – which had many points of contact with *Broken Arrow* – and knew the director slightly from the days when Mann had run a summer company at the Red Barn Theater on Long Island, where Stewart had worked briefly in 1934.

Even before a foot of film had been shot, *Winchester '73* had established itself as a landmark in Hollywood history on account of the deal that Stewart's agent, Lew Wasserman, negotiated on his behalf. Instead of being paid a flat fee, he was granted a 50% share in the profits. This wasn't entirely without precedent – some of the more impoverished studios such as RKO had been known to strike similar bargains – but it was certainly the first time that a major star like Stewart had specifically sought out the arrangement. It was a gamble, but it paid off handsomely: Borden Chase once claimed that the actor made more than a million dollars from the movie, and the real figure – about $600,000 – is scarcely less impressive. His earnings did pass the million-dollar mark, in fact, when he worked for the same percentage deal on *The Glenn Miller Story*, while his stake in the profits of Hitchcock's *Rear Window*, *The Man Who Knew Too Much* and *Vertigo* would ensure that he was still receiving hundreds of thousands of dollars from these films even in the 1980s, when they enjoyed a new lease of life in the cinema and on video. Other stars, naturally enough, were quick to jump on to the bandwagon, and if any one single factor can be said to have hastened the demise of the major studios, it would be the resulting precipitous decline in their long-term profits. (This makes Stewart's frequent laments about the collapse of the studio system sound somewhat ironic: rather like his complaints about the new permissiveness of the 1960s and '70s – failing to acknowledge that some of his own films, notably *Vertigo* and *Anatomy of a Murder*, had of course been instrumental in dragging the Hollywood cinema out of its over-prolonged state of innocence.)

As for *Winchester '73* itself, it turned out to be a marvellous movie which has some claim to be called the *Casablanca* of Westerns: partly because of the boost it gave to its star's ailing career, but also because, like the Bogart film, it single-handedly manages to encapsulate and revitalise almost every cliché of its genre. Several critics have pointed out the remarkable number of Western conventions the film incorporates within its brief running time: they include, among others, a family feud, a shoot-out, a saloon fight, a bank robbery, a poker game, a saloon-girl with a heart of gold, and an attack on the cavalry by marauding Apaches. Threading all these disparate elements together is the story of the 'real pretty' Winchester rifle – referred to as 'one of a thousand' and 'the gun that won the West' – as it passes between all the movie's various

WINCHESTER '73: the shooting contest which initiates a cycle of violence.

characters before ownership finally reverts to Lin McAdam, Stewart's obsessive hero, hell-bent on seeking vengeance for his father's murder.

With Shelley Winters.

Anthony Mann remembered *Winchester '73* as being 'one of my biggest successes, and also my favorite Western. The gun which passed from hand to hand allowed me to embrace a whole epoch, a whole atmosphere. I really believe that it contains all the ingredients of the Western, and that it summarizes them.' Part of its authenticity, he believed, came from Stewart's determination to look convincing when he handled the gun. 'He studied hard at it … He worked so hard his knuckles were raw with practising, so that he could be right. And we had an expert from the Winchester Arms Company who taught him how to really *uniquely* use the gun. These are the things that give it a sense of tremendous reality.' Equal care was taken over apparently minor details, such as the choice of Stewart's hat. 'It took us nearly two months to find the right hat for Jimmy Stewart … Since the hat is rarely taken off, not even in a house – and you never go inside one if you can help it – it's very important. If you don't get the right hat you may as well not get on a horse. John Wayne's a big man and he can wear a big hat. Jimmy is very slim and couldn't. Some of the tests we made were hysterical. Anyway, we eventually got him a hat full of holes and with a big, greasy sweatband. That hat got a great notice in the *New York Times*.'

For his own part, Mann was not surprised by the degree of violence and intensity that Stewart brought to the film. He always maintained, 'Within

Stewart gets tough in WINCHESTER '73. *'Within himself,' said Anthony Mann, 'he has something much more burning and exciting than when you meet him personally.'*

himself he has something much more burning and exciting than when you meet him personally. Stewart is a man who's devoted his whole life to acting and who's quite brilliant in what he does. He's very skillful and, once you start going with him, he's marvelous to work with because he's always there. He's always anxious: he wants to be great.' This 'anxiety' and driving sense of purpose find their most complete expression in the solitary, obsessed hero created for Stewart by Mann and Borden Chase. They can

sometimes leave him teetering on the edge of madness, the pursuit of his personal demon having become so dogged and unswerving that one of his companions will claim – as in *Winchester '73* – 'You're beginning to like it'. 'Well, that's where you're wrong,' Stewart answers. 'I don't like it. Some things a man has to do, so he does it.' With an amazing instinct for dramatic brinkmanship, he pushes the characterisation just as far as it can be taken without losing his grip on the audience's trust, so that we continue to root for Stewart even while feeling a measure of sympathy for the sidekick who observes warily, 'Sometimes I think he's a little on the crazy side.'

Stewart made three more films before his next collaboration with Anthony Mann, none of them very distinguished. *The Jackpot* was a pleasant but dispensable comedy about a harassed executive and family man who wins an enormous prize on a radio quiz show and then finds that horrendous complications ensue. After that, Stewart got a call from Henry Koster in England to say that Robert Donat (whose debilitating asthma cost him countless film parts over the years) had been obliged to drop out of a film called *No Highway*, and was he available to take over the part? It was an attractive proposition in many ways, offering the chance to return to the scene of his wartime experiences, to work on a film with an aeronautical subject, and to star opposite Marlene Dietrich once again. Stewart played the Rhodes scholar Theodore Honey, now a widower and working as a research scientist at the Royal Aircraft Establishment in Farnborough. At first, coming across as the classic absent-minded boffin, he seems the very opposite of *Winchester '73*'s embittered gunman; but like Lin McAdam, Honey is engaged upon a single-minded odyssey – in his case, a research project designed to prove that the Reindeer aircraft is unsafe and will break up from metal fatigue after a certain number of flying hours.

The film can be divided into three parts. The first shows us Honey's domestic life, alternating between broad comedy (he tries to go through the wrong front door on his own housing estate) and touching scenes with his daughter, wise beyond her years and beautifully underplayed by Janette Scott. In the second section, he is obliged to fly aboard a Reindeer himself, and midway through the journey becomes convinced that disaster is about to strike. This is a long, tense and quiet sequence, with Stewart doing a virtuoso turn – all shifting eyes and jittery hand movements – as the passenger burdened with

No Highway: explaining the laws of aerodynamics to an attentive Marlene Dietrich.

Stewart and Gloria showing off their twin daughters Kelly and Judy. Now aged forty-two, he had become a father for the first time.

terrible private suspicions. When they land for refuelling, he is so determined that the flight shouldn't be resumed that he sabotages the plane, and this initiates the film's third, rather preposterous section, in which the airline attempts to prove him insane, but the results of his own tests finally prove his sanity and his theory. In the meantime, he is given succour by a kindly air hostess (Glynis Johns) and a famous movie star and fellow-passenger (Dietrich).

Like Stewart, Dietrich took her film-making seriously. 'She knew the camera and knew what was right for her,' he said. 'She knew it so well that she could look up, before a scene, and say, "Would you move the key light up about two inches?" They'd look at each other and say, "Jeez, she's right!"' Yet it's hard to understand why she should have agreed to play this secondary and very implausible character. Henry Koster recalled that she was 'not very happy' making the film, and kept asking, 'Oh my God, aren't we through with this picture yet?' He knew that the part was unstimulating for her: 'She had to sit in an airplane and get upset about a crazy scientist, which isn't much of a display of a great actress. She did it well, though.'

While the Stewarts were staying in England, Gloria found that she was pregnant, and after flying home for tests she sent her husband a telegram to announce that she was expecting twins. (Their daughters, Kelly and Judy, were born on 7 May 1951.) At the same time, Stewart heard from Hollywood that Cecil B. DeMille was in the process of casting his circus extravaganza, *The Greatest Show on Earth*, and was looking for someone to play Buttons the clown. It was a small part, but Stewart's expression of interest was enough to persuade the director that it should be expanded considerably: 'After I finished *No Highway* and got back, I realized that DeMille had created a

Stewart returns to England on the Queen Elizabeth, *with Gloria and sons, for the filming of* No Highway.

whole sub-plot involving the character.' This sub-plot, it has to be said, is very silly indeed. It supposes that Buttons is, in fact, a doctor wanted by the police for the mercy killing of his wife and that he has disguised himself as a clown and joined the circus in order to escape arrest. (Well, you would, wouldn't you?) As for the film, it won the Best Picture Oscar in 1952 (the year of *The Quiet Man*) and at the end of the 1950s was ranked the ninth-highest moneymaker of all time. It is also monumentally tedious: only DeMille's leaden hand could have taken so much colour, drama and spectacle and transformed it into two and a half hours of insufferable dullness. Stewart, clowning and singing with the rest of the troupers, is perfectly acceptable in a part that could have been played by anybody. Asked why he had been so eager to do it, he answered cryptically, 'I'd always wanted to play a clown.'

After that, it can only be a relief to find him back in the saddle again for *Bend of the River*, with Anthony Mann directing and another fine, complex screenplay by Borden Chase. Nominally it was based on a novel by Bill Gulick called *Bend of the Snake*, which Stewart had optioned himself; but Chase took a cavalier approach to his source material. 'Jimmy goes out and buys books by the cover, he doesn't read the inside,' he explained. 'I said, "Jimmy, who do you see yourself as in this book? Did you read it?" He said, "Well, no, I read the jacket. Somebody told me it was good for me." I said, "Well, you take it home tonight and read it." So he did. He came in the next day and he said, "Well, what are we going to do with it?" And I threw it in the wastebasket. I said, "That's what we're going to do with it. I'll get you out of your expense of buying it, though, I'll use the title." I didn't want to use "snake" so I called it *Bend of the River*. And the guy that did write the book, when it was shown in Portland, he took out a full page ad and said, "The only thing of mine in this film is the first three words of the title – *Bend of the*."'

As Buttons the clown in The Greatest Show on Earth, *with Charlton Heston.*

Stewart played Glyn McLyntock, a former Missouri border raider who has now gone straight and has been hired to guide a band of settlers to the Oregon territory. He is joined by Emerson Cole (Arthur Kennedy), another former outlaw whose reformation is not quite so complete, and together

*DeMille directing Stewart, Betty
Hutton and Emmett Kelly. Kelly
was a famous circus clown and
Stewart had been anxious to do
the film largely for the chance to
work with him.*

A scene from BEND OF THE RIVER, *shot on location at Mount Hood, Oregon.*

Stewart gamely takes part in a local celebration off the set of BEND OF THE RIVER.

they embark upon the risky enterprise of transporting several wagonloads of winter supplies up to the settlers' camp, hotly pursued by a crooked supplier and his gang who had been hoping to resell them to a group of gold-miners at a much higher price. It's a fast, noisy, crowded, very intense and remarkably violent Western, with a cumulative body count that would not have disgraced Arnold Schwarzenegger in his most casually genocidal phase.

It's easier to admire the Stewart character here than in *Winchester '73*: his past may be dodgy but his determination to bring food to the settlers is presented in an almost saintly light – so much so that when he succeeds, the

Stewart's final ordeal in THE NAKED SPUR, crawling through the rapids with a broken leg. 'He likes to have to do these things,' Mann insisted.

film invites us to regard it as a triumphantly happy ending, in spite of the fact that it presumably means death by starvation for an entire settlement of blameless gold-miners who needed the supplies just as much. What dark side there is to his personality emerges only in one sudden spasm of uncontrolled rage – he is about to knife a man before his sweetheart brings him to his senses – and in the unspoken bond of understanding that links him to Arthur Kennedy, who is finally revealed as the film's unrepentant villain. But Stewart's challenge in this movie has more to do with triumphing over impossible physical odds than with subduing the demons in his own soul.

THE NAKED SPUR.

The Naked Spur, on the other hand (which he made immediately after *Carbine Williams*, a mediocre biopic about the inventor of a famous rifle), is the most relentlessly internalised of the Mann/Stewart Westerns. Not that the landscapes aren't as outstanding as ever, or brought into the same intelligent relationship with the foreground action, but the movie is, by comparison with *Bend of the River* at least, something of a chamber piece, concentrating as it does on the psychological interaction between only five main characters. Of these, Stewart is Howard Kemp, a ruthless bounty hunter whose only goal in life is to raise $5,000 to buy back the farm which his fiancée cheated him out of; Robert Ryan is Ben Vandergroat, the outlaw who represents his prize. In taking him captive, Stewart bites off more than he can chew, because Ryan is accompanied by a woman (Janet Leigh), and reluctantly the bounty hunter is obliged to take on two accomplices, a cashiered officer (Ralph Meeker) and an ageing, disillusioned prospector (Millard Mitchell). This dependence on the assistance of others is a sign of weakness for which the Stewart character is seen to hate himself throughout the film: again and again he will set himself difficult tasks – shinning up a rock face on a length of rope, for instance – for which he turns out to be physically unsuited. Waking up in the middle of the night with screaming fits, and reduced almost to crippledom by a bullet in his leg, Stewart gives one of his most agonised and unhappy performances in a movie that *Variety* predicted would prove 'too raw and brutal for some theatregoers'.

Borden Chase didn't write the screenplay for this one, and it could do with some of his humour and snap. Also, Stewart's redemption in the closing scene is just a little too pat: it's the old saved-by-the-love-of-a-good-woman syndrome again, whereas Chase always went for more realistically compromised and effortful resolutions. But the film has a certain formal precision in the way it explores the mutual destructiveness of four men reduced to their naked passions, and is probably Mann's best attempt, prior to *The Man from Laramie*, at capturing the spirit of classical tragedy which he sought to echo in his Westerns. *Bend of the River* and *The Naked Spur* are serious, meaty films which wear their pretensions lightly: perhaps this is why they aren't as well remembered or as widely discussed as other, more ponderous Westerns such as *Shane* and *High Noon* – both of which, incidentally, they out-performed at the box office.

Thunder Bay (1953) was Stewart's next film with Anthony Mann, but it found them both off form. 'Its story was weak,' according to the director, 'and we were never able to lick it.' In fact, it is not so much 'weak' as too thoroughly riddled with contradictions for audience sympathy ever to come into focus. Stewart plays a businessman, down on his luck, who arrives on the Louisiana Gulf Coast in 1946 and realises that there is untold wealth to be found in the oil-rich ocean bed. Unfortunately his ambitions in this direction just happen to spell death for the local fishing community, and in the resulting conflict it's none too easy to come down on Stewart's side: there's simply nothing admirable about his crusade, unless we are meant to be impressed by the entrepreneurial spirit at its most avaricious. In its way this is one of the most nakedly ideological of Stewart's films, and none of the several well-staged action sequences can make it attractive. Stewart plays the movie on a sustained note of grizzled, aggressive stridency (reaching its apogee in the scene where oil gushes over him amid hysterical screams of 'Thar she blows!') which does nothing to win affection for his character.

Quite the opposite is true of *The Glenn Miller Story*, which contains probably his most cuddly performance on film. Like *Mr Smith Goes to Washington* and *It's a Wonderful Life*, this is a movie fondly remembered by fans who cherish an uncomplicated image of Stewart as shy, decent, well-mannered and steeped in mythical all-American values. But it's also infinitely better than either of those films, and provides a far more authentic biography of a musician than anything we might have expected, given Hollywood's healthy track record of travesties in

As rigging boss Steve Martin in THUNDER BAY.

this area. Of course, it helped that there was a real musician in the title rôle, even if Stewart never did manage to learn the trombone. 'I was determined not to have trombone players say, "You were faking it, the slide wasn't in the right place for the tune you were playing." ' But Joe Yukl, the trombonist assigned to coach him, realised after only a few days that he had a hopeless case on his hands, so Stewart agreed to silence the instrument by plugging up the mouthpiece and to concentrate on learning the correct hand positions instead. 'We worked out the tunes I had to play with a series of photographs and with

With June Allyson in THE GLENN MILLER STORY. *She played his wife in three films and shared an easy rapport with him on screen.*

THE GLENN MILLER STORY.

the musician showing me the position of the slide, and how long it stayed there. He'd stand to one side of the camera. The music was up above the camera. I'd watch the position of his trombone and match it.' The results were unusually convincing: even in the exhilarating jam session in a jazz club alongside Louis Armstrong, Stewart looks thoroughly in command of himself, full of the intent, introspective alertness of the real musician.

Thematically, *The Glenn Miller Story* is not too far removed from the rest of Stewart's work with Anthony Mann, who felt that the purpose of the film was 'to tell the story of a man who is hunting something new and finally finds it'. In doing so some fairly drastic simplifications had to be made, but the film was at least dealing with a recent, well-remembered era and a musical 'sound' that audiences could be expected to recognise; the uproarious bathos that had often attended Hollywood's efforts to pictorialise the likes of Chopin and Rimsky-Korsakov was thereby largely avoided. Besides, Stewart is so unassuming when he sits down at the piano and tries out the first tentative chords of *Moonlight Serenade* that we can almost believe it happened that way. Equally impressive was Mann's awareness of the potentially fatal sentimentality lurking at the corners of this material, which he dodged by choosing to end the film on a bitter-sweet upbeat, with the widowed June Allyson hearing Miller's arrangement of her favourite tune, 'Little Brown Jug', for the first time. Allyson doesn't try to tug at the viewer's heartstrings, either: forty years on, her chirpy appeal remains miraculously unfaded. The same goes for the film, too – and the reason for that might be that there was nothing fake, in either case, about the winsome charm they offered up to the audience so openly.

As if to redress the balance for all this guileless warmth and sincerity, Mann and Stewart now moved on to *The Far Country*, their coldest, most ironic Western (not released until 1955, for some reason). Full of themes and situations familiar from the other movies scripted by Borden Chase, it gives the impression that writer and director, having already

THE GLENN MILLER STORY.

Glenn and Helen Miller celebrate their tenth wedding anniversary to the tune of 'Pennsylvania 6-5000'.

proved that they could handle this sort of material straight, now decided to treat it more along the lines of a black comedy. Stewart plays a cattle-driver whose herd is confiscated by a judge (John McIntyre) when he arrives in Oregon Territory. The laconic tone of the film is set by one of McIntyre's first remarks to Stewart: 'I'm gonna like you. I'm gonna hang you, but I'm gonna like you.' Even in the first scene, however, the viewer has already received a shock by being confronted not with one of Mann's typical expansive landscapes, but with a grotesquely unrealistic painted backdrop of snowcapped mountains. Similarly unbelievable sets crop up later as Stewart and his companion, Walter Brennan, trek up to an isolated township in Alaska, and Chase peppers the screenplay with peculiar details, like an irrelevant discussion about why cows have four stomachs, and a sign that hangs over a saloon advertising 'BEAR STEW' in large letters.

And yet it would be wrong to dismiss the film as a throwaway exercise: remarkably, it also manages to sustain a note of seriousness equal to any of the other Westerns. For one thing, it succeeds in reworking *Of Mice and Men* in a Western setting. Walter Brennan is the Lenny figure, the clinging, dependent companion both loved and resented by Stewart, whose garrulous simple-

Although an accomplished musician, Stewart never did master the trombone, but few actors could have looked so convincing when miming on stage alongside Louis Armstrong.

THE FAR COUNTRY.

mindedness will eventually lead to his own death and the collapse of their shared dream (exactly the same dream as the one cherished by Steinbeck's couple – retiring to a little farm in the country where they can live in trouble-free isolation from the rest of the world). *The Far Country* also dramatises the moral education of Stewart's character, who starts off as a self-interested loner and ends by learning a sense of social responsibility; and it contains a good final suspense sequence, as Stewart – whose approach is easily identified throughout the film by the tinkling bell attached to his horse's saddle – dupes the villains lying in ambush for him by sending the horse out alone. Here, as in all his other Westerns, Stewart was riding a horse called Pie which he had first picked out for *Winchester '73*. 'I just fell in love with the horse,' he said. 'And I *swear* we got to know each other. He would do things that I just have never seen in a horse … They'd put a mark down, just a piece of tape, and I swear that horse would look up, and I would start pulling back …. but I didn't have to. He *knew* where to stop.' Their rapport was never better demonstrated than in the key sequence from *The Far Country* when Pie had to do his solo spot as a decoy. 'I was told, "We want Pie to go across the road, right in front of the saloon. How do we do that?" And I said, "Well, I'll just tell Pie what I want him to do." And I just went one time with him. I said, "Just keep going – and I won't be on you. Just keep going – now, come back faster. Then, we'll do this once more." The assistant director came up and said, "How long are you going to talk to him?" And I said, "He's fine, he'll do it." So they shot it. And he did it. Perfect.'

After *The Far Country* Stewart made *Rear Window* for Alfred Hitchcock, and then went on to sponsor a project that brought his conservatism and pro-military sympathies very much to the fore. Ever since the war he had been an active member of the Air Force Reserve, and he now took advantage of his considerable clout in Hollywood to put together a movie that would glorify its activities. Mann was his collaborator again – albeit a slightly reluctant one this time, especially as the film had to be made with the full co-operation of the Air Force, who consequently exerted a good deal of influence over what went into it. *Strategic Air Command* stars Stewart as a baseball player who is resentful at the interruption of his career when the SAC calls him up for service; there's a good deal of cold-war paranoia about how necessary it is for the armed forces to be kept at the ready, even in peacetime, but little in the way of plot, and the film is both dull and objectionable despite Mann's often inspired photography of the skyscapes. June Allyson played Stewart's wife, and once again there is a genuine warmth and empathy between them which provides welcome relief from all the

The inimitably toothless Walter Brennan stands by while Stewart metes out his own brand of justice in THE FAR COUNTRY.

A portrait taken after his controversial promotion to Brigadier General. It was largely through Stewart's influence with the military that STRATEGIC AIR COMMAND got made.

lingering shots of military hardware. It was Stewart's last appearance alongside the woman with whom he had always seemed most comfortable on screen: with Margaret Sullavan he had been too close, too vulnerable; with Donna Reed in *It's a Wonderful Life* he had seemed to resent the intimacy as much as he was sustained by it; with Grace Kelly in *Rear Window* there would be too much comically unresolved friction; and there can be few heterosexual relationships as tortured or perverse as the one portrayed by Stewart and Kim Novak in

Vertigo. But the three films he made with Allyson remain about as close as the American cinema has ever come to making a case for the happily married couple without resorting to hollow sentimentality.

Stewart and Mann now made their last Western together – *The Man from Laramie*, which many consider their finest. 'I wanted to recapitulate, somehow, my five years of collaboration with Jimmy Stewart,' Mann said. 'That work distilled our relationship. I reprised themes and situations by pushing them to their extremes.' Certainly there is the sense, in Philip Yordan and Frank Burt's screenplay, that Stewart's character has now gone beyond the vengeful monomania of Borden Chase's scripts, been humanised and socialised by his ironic foray into *The Far Country*, and emerged still angry, still driven, but now with a gentler, more approachable side which prompts his latest sidekick (Wallace Ford taking the Walter Brennan rôle) to venture, 'I don't suppose we spoke ten words coming down here, but I feel that I know you, and I like what I know.'

Stewart's mission this time is to avenge the death of his brother at the hands of the Apaches, by tracking down the gun-runner who has been supplying them with repeating rifles. This brings him into conflict with a wealthy landowner (Donald Crisp), his weak, arrogant son (Alex Nicol) and his foster son and ranch manager (Arthur Kennedy). Nicol first comes upon Stewart digging up salt on his father's land, and he metes out a savage punishment – roping him, dragging him through a fire, then burning his wagons and shooting his mules; a gruelling enough sequence which is nevertheless topped a little later in the film when Nicol calmly shoots Stewart through the hand at point-blank range. Mann once recalled the vivid impression that this boundary-breaking outburst of violence made on contemporary audiences: 'You see the hand of Stewart, and you see the gun go to the hand of Stewart, you see the trigger being pulled, and at that moment of pulling, the camera whipped up to a close-up of Stewart, and a shot, and the agony. And everybody said … they saw the bullet hit the hand. Now they never did. It was one second late, but the movement of the camera gave them the shock which made them believe that the hand was blown.' Sure enough, it's a superb piece of editing – but even more startling is the high-pitched shriek emitted by Stewart, divesting himself of any shred of tough-guy dignity in order to convey the character's pain.

Mann was fond of justifying the violence in his films by pointing out that it

THE MAN FROM LARAMIE: Will Lockhart's baptism of fire.

had a precedent in classical tragedy. As a young man, he got his first theatrical experience working on local productions of Sophocles, and later he found himself drawn to the Western because 'The West is the one place audiences will accept the violence and passion of the classical writers'. This influence was never more apparent than in *The Man from Laramie*, in which a scattered handful of characters play out their primal drama against the backdrop of vast, empty landscapes (stunningly framed in CinemaScope compositions which are, of course, lost in today's TV and video versions). Making a Western version of *King Lear* was a much-discussed ambition which Mann was never able to realise, but this film already has strong overtones of Shakespeare's play, with its theme of an ailing patriarch dividing his affections unequally between rival descendants; and the scene where Crisp, having lost his eyesight, charges up on a horse firing wildly and ineffectually at Stewart has something of the horrific inevitability of the blinding of Gloucester.

Certainly these were extreme images to be coming out of Hollywood in the mid-1950s, but Stewart was prepared to co-operate to the full. 'He'll say, "Look, Tony, if you want me to be pulled through the fire, then I'll do it,"' said Mann. '"If you want me to fight under the horses' hooves, I'll do it." This is the kind of guy he is. He likes to have to do these things.' In each of these films, Mann chose to portray the Stewart hero as 'a man who had gone through so much that when the time came and he finally got there, he was not exalted, he was exhausted … I don't think I have ended any of my films with any kind of exaltation: it's really more tired – he's done the job and thank heavens it's done – that sort of feeling.' This idea is taken even further in *The Man from Laramie*, when Stewart finally confronts his nemesis and realises that he can't shoot him in cold blood, but pushes him aside with a disgusted cry of 'Get away from me'. It's a strong, uncompromising note on which to end one of the most distinguished actor/director collaborations in film history – one that had worked an amazing transformation on Stewart's career, lifting him out of his post-war doldrums and turning him into the fifties' top box-office draw.

Mann and Stewart never made another film together. The director first announced his plans for the Western *King Lear* in the late 1960s, shortly before his death, but by then it was John Wayne he wanted for the title rôle. 'Wayne could do the moments of silence beautifully,' he explained, before conceding, 'The words, of course, are another matter.'

The final confrontation in THE MAN FROM LARAMIE, framed by a spectacular landscape in characteristic Anthony Mann style.

5

HITCHCOCK'S STEWART: 'EVERYMAN IN BIZARRE SITUATIONS' 1954-1958

Stewart's first collaboration with Hitchcock had been an interesting misfire. While he had been just as intrigued by the technical aspects as anyone involved in the production, he was fundamentally out of tune with its spirit; for *Rope* is, after all, one of Hitchcock's chilliest films, fuelled only by a single-minded interest in formal experiment and by a macabre relish in the presentation of grisly material. But *Rear Window*, which Stewart began shooting in November 1953, shortly after his return from *The Far Country*'s Canadian locations, was a different matter altogether. Despite the fact that its plot managed to encompass a wife-murder and a decapitation, it turned out to be perhaps the director's warmest movie since *The Lady Vanishes*. The explanation for this must lie (although *auteur*ists will gnash their teeth) with its screenwriter: John Michael Hayes – like Launder and Gilliat, writers of *The Lady Vanishes* – had a background in comedy as well as suspense, and his collaboration with Hitchcock on four projects during the 1950s infected these films with a slightly uncharacteristic vein of humanity and good humour.

Stewart did not have to see the *Rear Window* screenplay to know that he wanted to do it; reading Hayes's brief initial treatment was enough, and if he felt that it was time for a change from Westerns, he could hardly have asked for a greater one. After three years of throwing punches and cantering about the wide-open plains, his rôle as L.B. Jeffries called for him to be immobilised in a wheelchair for the entire film, his left leg encased in a heavy plaster cast. Stewart plays a news photographer whose leg has been broken on an assignment, and his function, for the most part, is not to participate in but to observe the action, through various 'screens' formed by windows in the apartment building opposite the room where he now sits out his increasingly

Reunited with Hitchcock for the masterly REAR WINDOW.

bored and frustrated convalescence. From behind these windows, a number of stories begin to emerge: an attractive young woman doing her best to ward off a posse of insistent suitors, a lonely spinster drifting towards suicidal despair, and, at the heart of the film, a murderous salesman's plot to dispose of his hated wife.

Hitchcock was more sensitive than most directors to the cumulative baggage of associations which an established star can bring to a film. 'The *enormous* advantage in casting the star,' he told Peter Bogdanovich, 'is because of familiarity … The moment he gets into jeopardy, the audience reaction is much stronger than it would be if the actor were a character man, who might be more right for the part.' Stewart, in his opinion, could bring more of this 'familiarity' to bear than any other actor, and this made him 'a perfect Hitchcock hero, because he is Everyman in bizarre situations'. François Truffaut once picked up on this point, observing that 'the lifelike impact of a Hitchcock movie is based on a personality previously acquired by the actor in films by other directors. James Stewart brought the warmth of John Ford to Hitchcock films.' This is actually one of his less sensible remarks (since Stewart did not work with Ford until after his last picture for Hitchcock), but it's still the case that part of *Rear Window*'s power derives from the creative use it makes of Stewart's already established star persona. Since his success in Westerns, for instance, his physical image had undergone a radical change: audiences were now more accustomed to seeing him dressed in cowboy leathers looking sweaty, grizzled and unshaven than cutting a dapper figure in tuxedo or double-breasted suit. The film capitalises on this by making a strong visual contrast between Stewart and his exquisitely-dressed girlfriend (Grace Kelly). While Kelly floats into the room modelling a succession of glorious outfits 'right off the Paris plane', and even the local detective (Wendell Corey) shows up for the dénouement wearing black tie, Stewart slobs around in his loose-fitting pyjamas, drawling, scratching himself and haranguing Kelly boorishly for her chronic unsuitability as a roving photographer's spouse. In this way, his newly-acquired Western mannerisms mean that he can concisely evoke an entire lifestyle – rugged, adventurous, mannish and outdoor – which is comically pitted against Kelly's Park Avenue sophistication.

The film also acquires an extra layer of resonance through our awareness of Stewart's wartime bravery. Although he does finally come into violent

REAR WINDOW.

Relaxing with Kelly between takes; the opportunity to stretch his legs must have been welcome.

confrontation with the killer (Raymond Burr), the most painful and suspenseful moment in the film comes when Kelly has ventured daringly into Burr's apartment and is attacked by him – at which point the camera lingers not on their struggle but on Stewart's face as he watches, helpless and agonised. To be trapped in such a situation would be torture enough for anyone, but the audience knows how much worse it must be for Stewart – the man who proved, during the war, that he could not rest easy when there was a fight to be fought, who felt that he'd been 'asked to serve my country, and … it would be my duty to do so', even to the extent of having to modify himself physically in order to qualify for the task.

Even though Stewart gives one of his greatest performances in *Rear Window*, it remains, above all, a writer's and director's film. Hayes's screenplay is the most complex and multi-layered Hitchcock ever had to work with; the murder mystery and the story of Stewart and Kelly's antagonistic romance unfold in perfect equilibrium, while the narrative vignettes glimpsed in all the other apartments constitute a myriad tiny sub-plots, each throwing ironic light back on the film's principal themes of voyeurism and engagement, the guilty pleasures of watching and the moral responsibility to act. The film's tempo, its audacious use of fades, its meticulously-assembled soundtrack of city noises, snatches of conversation and musical fragments (easily overlooked when so much stress has been laid on its visual brilliance) show a master director working at the height of his powers; or as Hitchcock himself put it, 'About this time I felt that my batteries were really fully charged.' The mood of confidence on the set – a sense of cast and crew rising to meet fearsome technical challenges with cheerfulness and ingenuity – is probably best summed up in an anecdote told by Stewart when the film was re-released in 1983.

'The lighting for some shots really created a problem. One day there were several shots where the camera was behind me – that is to say, I was in the foreground and across the courtyard the action was in focus. Well, you've got a big depth-of-field problem with that. It would need twice the amount of light, so that the aperture could be kept small to keep everything in focus. Paramount took all the lights they had from all the stages not in use and it still wasn't enough, then they borrowed lights from Columbia and MGM, and finally they could do the shot; the heat was really intense. Suddenly, in the middle of it, the lights set off the sprinkler system, not just a section of it, but on all the stages, and we're not talking about little streams of water but torrents. Everybody stopped as we were plunged into wet darkness. But it never

With Grace Kelly and Wendell Corey as the sceptical detective.

The woman who sang too much in THE MAN WHO KNEW TOO MUCH.

fazed Hitchcock. He sat there and told his assistant to get the sprinklers shut off and then to tell him when the rain was going to stop, but in the meantime to bring him an umbrella.'

After making his final two films for Anthony Mann, Stewart teamed up with Hitchcock again for *The Man Who Knew Too Much*, a remake of the director's 1934 thriller. This was a costly production with a running time half as long again as the original film's, and while some critics have rightly pointed out that its characterisations are much richer, and that it can also be viewed as a commentary on tensions within the American nuclear family, these elements were included at the expense of narrative tension – and indeed plausibility. Stewart and his co-star Doris Day were required to play a middle-class, middle-aged, middle-American couple on holiday in Morocco, where their son gets kidnapped as part of a convoluted espionage plot which culminates in a celebrated assassination scene at London's Albert Hall. This is an early example of Stewart slipping into the lovable, slightly bumbling *paterfamilias* rôle he was later to reprise in three comedies for Henry Koster in the 1960s and his short-lived TV series *The Jimmy Stewart Show* in the 1970s: a characteristic scene here milks some cheerful humour out of his attempts to fit his gangly legs beneath a low-slung table in their Moroccan hotel.

Unfortunately the laughter induced by such moments is often eclipsed among younger audiences by the merriment that greets Doris Day's lusty rendition of 'Que Sera Sera', which recurs at key moments in the film and is not at all conducive to a mood of suspense. Quite why it was thought necessary to indulge her vocal abilities in this way remains a mystery (especially since Hitchcock fought against the casting of Julie Andrews in *Torn Curtain* ten years later on the grounds that 'she was a singer'). It's a shame, because Day's

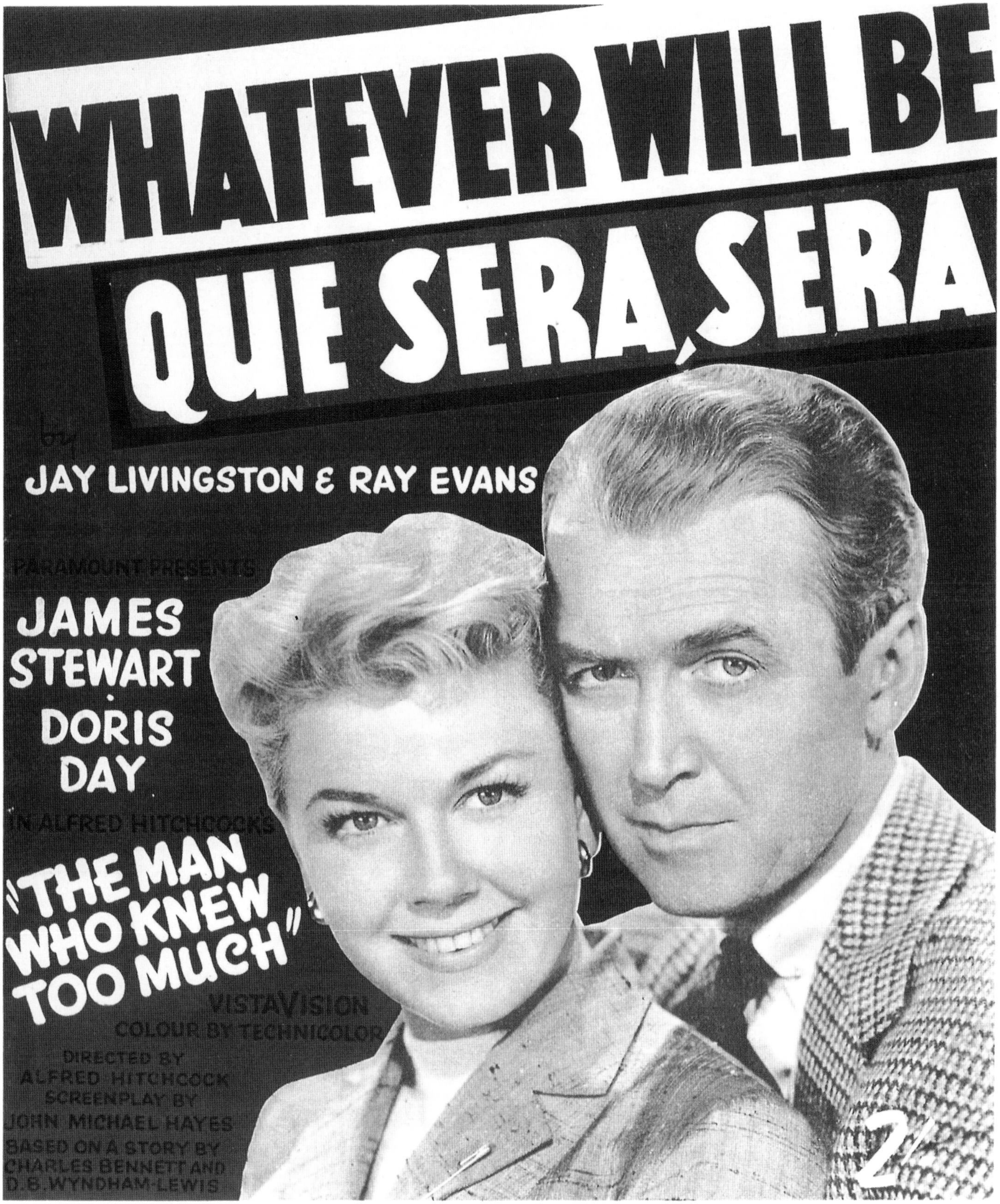
WHATEVER WILL BE
QUE SERA, SERA
by
JAY LIVINGSTON & RAY EVANS
PARAMOUNT PRESENTS
JAMES STEWART
DORIS DAY
IN ALFRED HITCHCOCK'S
"THE MAN WHO KNEW TOO MUCH"
VISTAVISION
COLOUR BY TECHNICOLOR
DIRECTED BY ALFRED HITCHCOCK
SCREENPLAY BY JOHN MICHAEL HAYES
BASED ON A STORY BY CHARLES BENNETT AND D.B. WYNDHAM-LEWIS
2/

Hitchcock and Stewart
collaborating for the third time,
with help from Bernard Miles,
Doris Day and Brenda de Banzie
(hidden).

performance is otherwise very good. She was ill at ease throughout the making of the film, mistaking the director's habitual taciturnity for unspoken resentment and disapproval; and so it was left to Stewart, as attentive towards his leading lady as ever, to take her aside and explain that Hitchcock always behaved like that. 'In the beginning,' he said, 'it certainly threw Doris for a loop. Doris surprised a lot of people with her acting in *The Man Who Knew Too Much*, but she didn't surprise Hitch, who knew what to expect from her. A singer's talent for phrasing, the ability to put heart in a piece of music, is not too far removed from acting, in which the aim is to give life and believability to what's on paper.' Fresh from his experience on *Rear Window*, Stewart was now in a good position to reassure other members of the cast about Hitchcock's idiosyncrasies. Bernard Miles, who played one of the villains, remembered that the director 'certainly did not annoy his cast with excessive attention', but felt better when Stewart told him, 'We're in the hands of an expert here. You can lean on him. Just do everything he tells you, and the whole thing will be okay.'

'Okay' is in fact a very fair description of *The Man Who Knew Too Much*; it provides a good deal of uneven fun on a single viewing, but essentially it's minor Hitchcock and minor Stewart. It was, nevertheless, one of the biggest moneymakers of its year, in marked contrast to Stewart's next picture, *The Spirit of St Louis*, which was once referred to by Jack Warner as 'the most disastrous failure we ever had'. And yet at first, it must have seemed that this project had success written all over it. The story of Charles Lindbergh's historic transantlantic flight was, surely, tailor-made for Stewart, with his proven ability to impersonate great American heroes, distinguished war record and long-standing interest in aviation. (An interest, incidentally, that showed no signs of abating: in 1958 he would break the sound barrier in a TF102–A Delta Dagger.) The only serious problem was the age difference: Lindbergh was twenty-five at the time of his flight, and Stewart was now forty-eight. But he worked hard to convince director Billy Wilder that he should be given the part, and was finally offered it when John Kerr turned it down. Kerr's reservations are said to have centred around the pro-Nazi sympathies Lindbergh had shown during World War II: for Stewart, who always seems to have found it remarkably easy to divorce acting from politics, this doesn't appear to have merited consideration.

The leading actor's age was only one of the difficulties that plagued the

Conferring with cinematographer Robert Burks on one of the windswept locations for THE SPIRIT OF ST LOUIS.

movie. There was the spiralling expense of the production (Lindbergh's original plane, for example, had cost $13,000 to build: Warner Brothers' replicas cost more than ten times that amount). There was Billy Wilder's inexperience with aerial photography; it may have been one of his most deeply cherished projects, but he had no appetite for this sort of location work, and recalled that 'We had unbelievable mechanical problems. We could not communicate with a plane when it was up there, so when we had to do another take, it had to land, get the instructions, and take off again. We had other

Right: Audience credulity was stretched to the limit when Stewart took on the part of the twenty-five-year-old Lindbergh.

As Charles Lindbergh in THE
SPIRIT OF ST LOUIS.

planes in the air to film the plane we were shooting. The weather would change from one minute to the next. God, it was horrendous.' And there was, most damagingly of all, the basic lack of dramatic interest in the story. Having decided to concentrate entirely on the transatlantic flight – rather than making the film a conventional biopic in the *Glenn Miller Story* mould – Wilder and Stewart found themselves saddled with the problem of holding the audience's interest throughout a two-hour monologue, and the best they could come up with was the idea of having Lindbergh talk to a fly which had found its way into the cockpit with him. (Asked whether his star might find this device a little undignified, Wilder answered, 'Mr Stewart does not object to talking to insects. After all, he has had to deal all his life with agents and producers.')

Lindbergh had been one of Stewart's idols ever since, at the age of nineteen, he had followed the original flight with a model plane and a map in the window of his father's store. As always, he brought considerable intelligence and professionalism to the part, and was personally congratulated by the aviator on one detail – tapping the oil gauge as he started the engine, which only an experienced pilot would think of doing. The film certainly looked beautiful, too, and was marvellously scored by Franz Waxman. But commercially it was a huge flop, largely because the title meant nothing to audiences, who seemed to be anticipating some sort of musical. Warner Brothers lost more than six million dollars on the movie, and in the week it opened in Lindbergh's home town, the local cinema did not even take enough money to pay its staff's wages.

Throughout the 1940s and '50s, Stewart filled in the gaps between films with radio and television appearances. Here he stars with Ann Harding and Cecil B. DeMille in the Lux Radio Theater production of MADAME X.

Further box-office ignominy awaited Stewart with *Night Passage*, an indifferent Western which Anthony Mann was earmarked to direct until he saw Borden Chase's script and pulled out in a hurry, grumbling about its predictability and incoherence. This led to a long-term rift between director and star, for Stewart chose to stay with the movie, apparently for little other reason than that it provided an opportunity to sing and play the accordion in two musical interludes. In any case, it gave him something to do while he waited for Alfred Hitchcock to sort out the long-term script problems on the film that would mark their last, and greatest, collaboration: *Vertigo*.

While *Vertigo* is generally (and rightly) regarded as Hitchcock's most personal film, people have tended to overlook the fact that Stewart himself took an unusually strong interest in its development. He read all the various early drafts of the screenplay, and so close was his involvement in pre-production that it had to be halted for several weeks in the winter of 1956-57, at Gloria's request, so that the family could take an extended holiday. Stewart agreed that Hitchcock had found what was potentially a 'fascinating story' in the novel *D'Entre les Morts* by Boileau and Narcejac (authors of *Les Diaboliques*), which concerned a detective – later renamed John 'Scottie' Ferguson – who falls obsessively in love with the beautiful woman he is assigned to follow. But he read the successive adaptations of it with increasing despair: first a confused, flowery one by Maxwell Anderson called *Darkling I Listen*, then a lifeless version by Alec Coppel under the more faithful title *From Amongst the Dead*. In both of these treatments Stewart found the characters 'completely unreal'. Meanwhile, Hitchcock was filling in his time shooting episodes of his TV show and Stewart did a bit of work in that area himself; he starred in *The Town with a Past*, a half-hour play for a series called *G.E. Theater*, hosted by Ronald Reagan, and then, for the first and only time in his career, tried his hand at directing, with *The Trail to Christmas*, a Westernised version of *A Christmas Carol*, for which he also provided the narration.

Finally, almost a year after *Vertigo* had been announced, the film's third writer, Samuel Taylor (who was, crucially, a native of San Francisco where Hitchcock had decided to relocate the action), managed to lick the screenplay into shape: his first contribution was to introduce Midge, the character played by Barbara Bel Geddes, who acts as a down-to-earth female foil to Stewart's tormented detective. 'I told Hitchcock immediately that I would have to invent

Stewart and Novak became good friends, even though he recalls being 'alarmed when I saw her first – this great big busty blonde, twice the weight I was'.

Midge (Barbara Bel Geddes), a new character written into the VERTIGO *story by Samuel Taylor, tries in vain to revive the broken-hearted Scottie.*

a character who would bring Scottie into the world, establish for him an ordinary life, make it obvious that he's an ordinary man.' As soon as Stewart read this new version, according to Taylor, he 'burst into Hitch's office at Paramount and said, "Well, at last these are real people – now we have a movie, now we can go ahead!"'

Casting had proved another stumbling block. Hitchcock had wanted Vera Miles for the crucial part of Madeleine, the object of Stewart's craving, but she had infuriated him by opting to have a baby instead. Ironically it took so long for the film to get off the ground that by the time shooting started, the child had been born and Miles could easily have been used after all; but Hitchcock was not one to forgive a snub, and besides, he had by now been persuaded – with some difficulty, at first – to cast Kim Novak in the rôle. He never spoke very highly of Novak's contribution to the film, and once said that the only good thing about it was that 'At least I got the chance to throw her into the water'. (He demanded multiple – some say gratuitous – retakes for the scene where she jumps into San Francisco Bay.) Stewart, who has never gone along with theories about Hitchcock's 'dark side', remembers this differently: 'I don't know whether he tested Kim for the part, but she worked out very well, contrary to rumor. Hitchcock thought so. In fact, it was the best thing she ever did. I got to know Kim very well, and I know that it was not true that Hitchcock gave her a hard time. She enjoyed the film enormously.'

Like many of the very greatest films, *Vertigo* is open – and has been subjected – to a variety of different interpretations, but the appeal it seems to hold most strongly for modern viewers (and male viewers in particular) is as a tragic exploration of the manipulativeness of masculine desire. The plot ostensibly centres on a murder mystery: Madeleine, the woman whom Stewart has been assigned to trail, appears to commit suicide; he meets another woman, Judy, who bears a close resemblance to her, and he tries to remake her in Madeleine's image only to discover, finally, that Judy and Madeleine are one and the same, and that he has been made the dupe of a scheme by an old college friend, Gavin Elster, to dispose of his wife. Anyone who looks only for conventional thriller elements in this movie comes away disappointed, however. The 'twist' is revealed two-thirds of the way into the film, and from then on it concentrates with stifling intensity on the power relationship between Scottie and Judy, as she succumbs more and more reluctantly to his attempts to clothe her in Madeleine's image, and Stewart hauls himself over the emotional coals, simultaneously appalled by the way he is treating her and driven on by his compulsive need to recreate the dead woman. Throughout this last section, Stewart and Novak have the screen entirely to themselves, the only other characters of any stature, Midge and Gavin Elster, having been perfunctorily abandoned along the way. (Interestingly, however, the final desolate image of Stewart standing alone on the bell-tower was *not* intended to be the last in the film. Another scene was shot, in which Scottie and Midge were shown together listening to the radio at night and hearing an announcement that Elster had been captured and arrested. This scene was even part of the release print in some countries.)

Vertigo has been analysed as a brilliant work of self-examination on Hitchcock's part, a commentary on the nature of illusion and therefore cinema itself. Much has also been written about Bernard Herrmann's score – perhaps the most memorable and influential ever to come out of Hollywood – which, with its tortured gravitation towards the elusive tonal centre of D major,

Vertigo: 'Scottie' Ferguson rescues Madeleine after an apparent suicide attempt.

*Stewart and Hitchcock
collaborated closely on the film,
even in its earliest stages.*

perfectly mirrors the central character's quest for emotional wholeness. The only key element in the film that has been under-praised, in fact, is Stewart's own performance. In part, this is a consequence of Hitchcock's long-term strategy of playing down the contributions made by actors to the success of his films. 'All actors are cattle' was one of his more notorious judgments, and Stewart, good-natured to the last, was prepared to see his point. 'I don't know how he got the reputation for saying that,' he recalled. 'But he did correct himself: "I never said actors were like cattle – I just said they should be *treated* like cattle." This seemed to Hitchcock to take all the sting out of the remark. But … when you come right down to it, it's not such an insulting thing. You're told to go there, to go here, to turn right, and if you're not doing it fast enough, he'll push you. So I don't think I mind the reference.'

All the same, we should be wary of giving Hitchcock all the credit for *Vertigo*'s tremendous emotional impact. Take, for instance, the famous reverse zoom he uses to convey Scottie's acrophobia in the bell-tower scene. True, it's a shocking, powerful device which jerks the viewer into identification: but isn't the real extent of the character's agony at this point expressed in Stewart's face, his catches of breath, the unconscious way he gnaws at his shaking hand? Similarly, in the climactic moment at Novak's hotel, as he waits for Judy to reappear with the final adjustment to her hair that will mark her complete transformation into Madeleine, Hitchcock's audacious use of colour – the whole room bathed in the nauseous green of a neon light from the street outside – adds immeasurably to our sense of Stewart's sickness: but is there in fact anything more moving in this scene than the look in his eyes – pale, beseeching and swelling with frantic tears? In this film he brought to the screen – without any recourse to histrionics – emotional states more extreme than any that had previously been portrayed in mainstream cinema. (One thinks, in particular, of the near-catatonic Stewart of the sanatorium sequence, looking old and fragile in his thin cardigan.) It's a performance that would leave a permanent mark: the hardness etched on to his face in the closing scenes, the frown lines and the angry beetling of the brows, became a familiar, discouraging feature of Stewart's screen appearance throughout the 1960s. A career-crowning performance, in other words, one that he was never likely to surpass, and which must have raised in his mind a disturbing question: where next?

6

WRESTLING WITH REALITY
1958-1993

In the short term, at least, the answer to that question was not long coming: in return for securing Kim Novak's services in *Vertigo*, Paramount had agreed to loan Stewart out to Columbia so that he could star in another picture with her. This was *Bell, Book and Candle*, a supernatural comedy which cast Stewart as a publisher and Novak as a witch who uses her magical powers to win his affections. Based on a long-running stage hit starring Rex Harrison, it turned out to be a charming, frothy time-passer with good support from the young Jack Lemmon as Novak's brother. All concerned seem to have had good fun making it; but at the same time, there were a couple of things weighing on Stewart's mind.

One of them was his anxiety to be given the lead in Hitchcock's next film, *North by Northwest*. When the director ignored his pleas and assigned it to Cary Grant – as had always been his intention – Stewart was bitterly disappointed. And meanwhile, he was doing his best to ignore an unexpected and very public controversy surrounding his war record, of all things. In 1957 it had been announced that he was to be promoted to Brigadier General in the Air Force Reserve, but the promotion was opposed by a Republican Senator, Margaret Chase Smith, who claimed that in the eleven years since his return to civilian life, Stewart had put in only nine days of active service. It took two years for the argument to be resolved, during which time Stewart did another fifteen days' training and agreed to a downgrading which meant that in the event of mobilisation, he would become Deputy Director of Information rather than Operations. (It was a switch to public relations, in other words.) Once this was settled the promotion was finally waved through by the Senate, but much of the glory had been lost and the incident must have been deeply

A frail General Sternwood in Michael Winner's THE BIG SLEEP.

hurtful to Stewart, who has remained tight-lipped on the subject ever since.

Up until now, after all, he had enjoyed a near-perfect relationship with press and public alike, but he now also fell foul of the more strait-laced wing of his fan club when he signed up for Otto Preminger's *Anatomy of a Murder*, in which he played Paul Biegler, a country attorney defending an army lieutenant (Ben Gazzara) on trial for murdering the man who is alleged to have raped his wife. In trying to establish whether or not the rape took place, Stewart found himself using words that would previously have been unthinkable in a Hollywood movie – words like 'sperm', 'contraceptive' and 'climax' – and having to hold up a torn pair of women's panties in the courtroom as evidence. When the film was released he was deluged with mail from outraged ex-admirers accusing

ANATOMY OF A MURDER: Stewart as a small-town lawyer, Lee Remick as his client's flirtatious wife.

In BELL, BOOK AND CANDLE, his second film with Kim Novak.

All lawyers are essentially actors, Stewart decided, while researching his part in ANATOMY OF A MURDER, and, as if to prove his point, a real lawyer (Joseph N. Welch) was called in to play the judge after the rôle had been turned down by Spencer Tracy and Burl Ives.

him of having betrayed his traditional family audience. Back home in Indiana, his father slipped into his most formidably authoritarian mode and even placed a notice in the window of the hardware store advising his customers to boycott this 'dirty movie'. (At this stage, however, he hadn't seen the film himself; when he did, he removed the notice.)

Thirty years on we might wonder what the fuss was about, since nothing dates faster than yesterday's attempts to be controversial. *Anatomy of a Murder* followed on naturally enough from the earlier films (*The Moon Is Blue, The Man with the Golden Arm*) in which Preminger had attempted to smuggle risky material into mainstream cinema, but in fact these ventures were all rather timid. Everything here, for instance, is done under the impeccable cover of legal procedure and terminology, and who would dare to complain about a movie that was not only based on a novel by a judge, but even cast a judge – Joseph N. Welch, a high-profile Boston lawyer with famously anti-McCarthyite leanings – in the central rôle of a presiding magistrate? Yet all this recourse to legal authority still can't hide the fact that the film's attitude towards rape is not at all progressive. Absurdly, we are supposed to believe that it's the *man* who is so upset by his wife's ordeal that he has to go out and murder somebody; as for the woman (Lee Remick), she seems remarkably cheerful and untraumatised – apart from a nasty black eye which clears up after a day or two. Besides, just about everyone (Stewart included) seems to assume that if it can be proved she went out that night without her panties on, the whole case will collapse because she must have been 'asking for it'.

On the positive side, the film is admirably equivocal in its portrayal of Gazzara, who is never made to seem particularly likeable; in a cheeky pay-off, he and Remick clear out of town when the case is over, leaving behind only an impudent note and an unpaid bill. This ambivalence reflects back on Stewart's character, who is never quite convinced of his client's innocence and is therefore prepared to acknowledge the element of play-acting in his own conduct of the defence. 'As the defense lawyer I knew I had to be glibber than usual,' Stewart recalled. 'Trial lawyers are neither shy nor inarticulate.' This puts a little ironic gloss on the country-boy mannerisms, the hemming and hawing and sudden bursts of righteous indignation which are so familiar from his other films but which he deploys here with an element of professional calculation. George C. Scott had his first major part as the prosecuting counsel and was astonished by Stewart's generosity as an actor: when doing his close-ups, Scott expected to be fed his cues by a stand-in as usual, but found that Stewart himself not only was willing to do it but even turned up *in costume* to make it easier for Scott to feel his way into the situation. (This generosity seems to have been based on real esteem: Scott's performance in *Patton* was one of the few things Stewart could find any praise for in the 1970s.) Though it has its longueurs, the combination of Stewart's knowing and complex characterisation, Scott's electrifying début and a weirdly appropriate score by Duke Ellington raises *Anatomy of a Murder* well above the level of the other innumerable courtroom dramas that have followed in its wake.

In marked contrast – and as if to foreshadow the erratic course his career would take in the future – Stewart now went straight on to *The FBI Story*, perhaps his most reactionary movie and one that it would be pleasing to regard as a temporary aberration. This hagiographic account of the noble war waged by Federal Agents against the Bolshevik meanies didn't even have brevity on its side, clocking in at a lumbering two and a half hours. Audiences liked it, though – far more than they liked the arguably more interesting *The Mountain Road*, an unusually grimy anti-war movie in which Stewart stepped well out of character as a brutal officer waging war against the Japanese in 1944 (and destroying an entire Chinese village in the process).

It was time to return to the West: but not, this time, to the West of Anthony Mann's neo-classical dramas. Stewart and Mann, after all, had come to the Western together – each with only a couple of films in this genre behind him – and had charted a course through its possibilities side by side. But by the time Stewart got round to working with John Ford, the director had already made his greatest Westerns and was ready to embark upon a more questioning, revisionist phase. Its first manifestation came with *Two Rode Together*, in which Stewart was cast as Guthrie McCabe, a cynical, mercenary town marshal who is hired by the Cavalry to rescue white prisoners held captive by the Comanches. Ford didn't care much for the story, feeling that he had already covered this ground in *The Searchers*, but agreed to do it 'as a favor to Harry Cohn' – although not graciously: 'I said, "OK, I'll do the damn thing." And I didn't enjoy it. I just tried to make Stewart's character as humorous as possible.'

'Humour', of course, is the one thing that was lacking from Stewart's characterisations in the Anthony Mann films, and *Two Rode Together* turns out

THE FBI STORY.

to be an even more laconic Western than *The Far Country*. It depicts a world where the governing values are to be found in downbeat comedy, casual misogyny, and a take-it-or-leave-it attitude to human life: all of them epitomised in the famous five-minute two-shot of Stewart and Richard Widmark sitting on a riverbank bantering about money, women and the Comanche problem in one unrehearsed, semi-improvised take. Ford justified this scene in terms of a simple preference for two-shots over close-ups: 'We've got this big screen: instead of putting a lot of pock-marked faces on it … if I can play a scene in a two-shot, where you can see both faces very well, I prefer it that way. You see people instead of just faces.' A different explanation has been put forward by those who were present when the scene was filmed – including Stewart himself: Ford was so bad-tempered during the making of this movie, they have claimed, that it amused him to have the crew wade out into the icy river early in the morning and stay there until the long take was completed.

Two Rode Together is not a likeable or satisfactory film and Stewart's performance, curiously, seems almost *too* relaxed – as if he hasn't fully grasped the moral emptiness of his character and is happy to play him as nothing more than a wisecracking rogue. He would be far better served by Ford's next film, *The Man Who Shot Liberty Valance*, which was a more committed and thoughtful examination of the values upon which the American West was built. In it he plays Ranson Stoddard, an idealistic young student determined to bring law and order to the town of Shinbone, in order to combat the rampant, trigger-happy individualism of Liberty Valance (Lee Marvin). Having trouble setting up as an attorney in a town where most of the population can't read, Stewart resorts to washing dishes, and soon falls for his Swedish helpmate, Hallie (Vera Miles). His rival for Hallie's affections, Tom Doniphon (John Wayne), is convinced that Valance will never be brought to book, and that if Stewart is going to defeat him, he'll have to learn how to use a gun. But Stewart believes that justice, freedom and progress can be achieved through constitutional means – shades of Thomas Jefferson Destry, here – and sets about instructing the townsfolk in the virtues of literacy and democracy.

This conflict has a deeply ironical outcome: having killed Valance in a gunfight, Stewart becomes a hero and the elected representative of his people on the basis of his reputation as 'the man who shot Liberty Valance' – but he then learns that it was Wayne's bullet all along. The film can be read, then, as a

*John Wayne as Tom Doniphon,
Stewart as Ranson Stoddard in
THE MAN WHO SHOT LIBERTY
VALANCE.*

TWO RODE TOGETHER: *Guthrie McCabe negotiates a fee for his services with Major Frazer (John McIntire).*

With director John Ford.

Politics and violence intersect to ironical effect in The Man Who Shot Liberty Valance. _Stewart is supposedly playing a character in his twenties._

strongly anti-pacifist polemic: 'civilised' values are all very well, but it takes a real gunslinger like Wayne to defend them (_and_ he won't get any credit for it). Its famous tag-line – 'This is the West, sir: when the legend becomes fact, print the legend' – was endorsed by Ford ('It's good for the country to have heroes to look up to') and frequently used by Stewart, throughout the late sixties and seventies, as a stick with which to beat the new realism of the post-Spaghetti Westerns. As a political position it may be reprehensible – offering a blueprint, in effect, for all manner of chicanery and cover-ups – but _The Man Who Shot Liberty Valance_ itself at least has the honesty to recognise the emotional devastation visited upon people who are obliged to live with the knowledge of such a lie: this is apparent from its final shots of an ageing Vera Miles, obviously still in love with Wayne and heartbroken by her return to Shinbone on the occasion of his funeral. (He has died unmarried and unremembered.) Stewart here is imbued with a new kind of ambiguity. As the youthful idealist in the main body of the film he is back to his Destry or Mr Smith mode (stretching it a bit at the age of fifty-four), but as the elder statesman revisiting Shinbone in the film's opening and closing sequences, he allows us to see what that figure has become. We realise now that this honoured patriarch, standing for all that is noble about American public life, has based his authority upon a lie, a shamefaced elevation of the 'legend' over truth which has brought untold pain to two of the people closest to him.

Before his final part in Ford's revisionist trilogy, Stewart would be involved with some less interesting projects. _How the West Was Won_ was an all-star, multi-

As Guthrie McCabe in Two
Rode Together.

director compendium filmed in a cumbersome three-screen format called Cinerama which makes it all but unwatchable on video or television today. Stewart was in the first episode, 'The Rivers', playing a wild trapper or 'mountain man' and looking most uncomfortable in his Daniel Boone outfit. He has to confess at one point to being 'deep dark sinful': 'I'm on my way to Pittsburgh to be sinful again. Likely I'll stay drunk for a month, I won't even remember the fancy gals I dally with and the men I carve up, just out of pure cussedness.' The lack of conviction this lifelong Presbyterian brings to the rôle of long-haired reprobate is quite woeful. Meanwhile, at the other extreme, he embarked upon a trio of painfully mild and wholesome comedies under the direction of his old friend Henry Koster. *Mr Hobbs Takes a Vacation* (1962), *Take Her, She's Mine* (1963) and *Dear Brigitte* (1965) each cast him as a befuddled but lovable father figure trying to cope with the vagaries of his wayward children.

Right: As wild 'mountain man' Linus Rawlings in HOW THE WEST WAS WON.

Stewart, Sandra Dee and Philippe Forquet making their own personal contribution to sixties kitsch in TAKE HER, SHE'S MINE.

A cynical Wyatt Earp in John Ford's CHEYENNE AUTUMN.

To give these films youth appeal, the children were played by hot teenage stars of the day such as Sandra Dee and the now forgotten Fabian; in the case of *Dear Brigitte,* even more desperate measures were taken and *la Bardot* herself was roped in for a guest appearance. Stewart has looked back on the making of these films with affection, while remaining too shrewd a critic of his own work to make any great claims for their quality. They certainly tell us nothing we didn't already know about his comic abilities, which were now also being given a regular airing on television: the Stewarts' annual guest appearance on *The Jack Benny Show,* for instance, was rapidly becoming institutionalised.

'Recently,' Stewart wrote in 1975, 'there has been a vogue for a new kind of "realistic" Western – a Western that tells us Jesse James was a coward, Wyatt Earp a drunk. They seem very petty and unimportant to me. Why try to destroy something that has been vital to people for so long?' And yet there can be few films that have debunked the myths of the Old West quite as scathingly as the notorious 'Battle of Dodge City' sequence in John Ford's *Cheyenne Autumn* (1964), which found Stewart himself playing Wyatt Earp as a self-obsessed gambler, deaf to the demands of the people he is supposed to be protecting. Quite what this piece of knockabout comedy is doing in the middle of a solemn treatise about the mistreatment of native Americans has always been open to argument. It was a very important film to Ford, who had come to feel himself guilty of great errors of omission and emphasis in this area, partly because he had always believed that to portray native Americans with dignity would be 'not very popular in the United States. The audience likes to see Indians get killed. They don't consider them as human beings, with a great culture of their own, quite different from ours.' If the Dodge City scenes – a fifteen-minute sequence in the middle of the film, quite unconnected to the main action – are meant to reflect back on the nobility of the dispossessed Cheyenne by portraying the white man as venal and uncaring, the ploy misfires, because this sequence (by virtue of its sheer weirdness, apart from anything else) is by far the most entertaining in the film, and only shows up the lifelessness and the lack of imaginative energy brought by Ford to the Cheyenne scenes. Warners were baffled by it, in any case, and cut the last few minutes – in which Stewart encourages his townspeople to escape the advancing Cheyenne by the brave expedient of running in the opposite direction – thereby obscuring whatever satiric point it may have had. (The full version has now been restored for the film's American video release.)

Ford's last three Westerns show that even this director, one of the greatest – as well as one of the most politically reactionary – exponents of the genre, now realised that this particular cinematic seam could not be mined for much longer. But Ford, who was nearing the end of his career, could afford to throw in the towel at this point, whereas for Stewart, with a good many years' film-making in front of him, the Western was still his bread and butter. And so he began a four-film association with Andrew V. McLaglen, the son of Victor McLaglen, one of Ford's regular players, and a self-styled inheritor of the Ford mantle. Their first film together, *Shenandoah*, was in fact Stewart's biggest moneymaker of the 1960s. This is rather surprising, given that today it seems such a low-key, thoughtful, literate movie, but perhaps its emphatic anti-war message struck a chord at a time when America was in a deep crisis of conscience over Vietnam. Stewart played Charlie Anderson, widowed head of a family of five sons and one daughter, who is determined to stay neutral in the Civil War which is raging on the doorstep of his Virginia farm. His performance is solemn and dignified, but by no means one of his liveliest, and this is perfectly in keeping with the rest of the film, which boasts a very well-written screenplay but little in the way of flair – or indeed any kind of visual style that it can call its own. (It has the look, to be honest, of an episode from a sixties Western TV series like *The Virginian* or *The High Chaparral*.) Towards the end of the film Stewart delivers a famous speech about the futility of war. Standing over his wife's grave, he says, 'I don't even know what to say to you, Martha. There's nothing much I can tell you about this war. It's like all wars, I suppose: the undertakers are winning it, politicians talk a lot about the glory of it, but the soldiers – they just want to go home.' All very fine and noble – but a tad ironic coming from a public figure who was by now firmly associated with

Stewart as the neutral, peace-loving patriarch Charlie Anderson in SHENANDOAH – seen here with Pie, the horse he rode in every one of his Westerns from WINCHESTER '73 onwards.

Right: *On the set of* SHENANDOAH. *The cigar is a prop: Stewart himself has never smoked.*

the American military establishment and increasingly given to approving statements about the US presence in Vietnam. (He didn't confine himself to speaking on the subject, either. Stewart made three trips to Vietnam during the war: as a member of the Air Force Reserve, he took part in a B-52 mission to Guam, on a target ten miles east of the Cambodian border, not far from Saigon; he went over again on an inspection tour, and then on another tour in 1968, the year of his retirement from the army.)

Immediately after *Shenandoah* he turned in what is perhaps the last of his great performances, as Captain Frank Towns in Robert Aldrich's *The Flight of the Phoenix*. It was Gloria who had recommended that he read Elleston Trevor's novel, which described a plane crash in the middle of the Sahara and the efforts of the survivors to build a new plane from the wreckage and fly it to safety. Clearly it appealed to his own flying instincts, and when he heard that Robert Aldrich owned the movie rights it seemed natural that they should collaborate. A strong, largely British supporting cast was assembled, including Richard Attenborough, Peter Finch, Ian Bannen and Ronald Fraser. Aldrich's son, who attended rehearsals, recalled that Stewart was at first quite intimidated by this company, and was embarrassed that on the first day 'everyone knew his lines and Jimmy didn't. It was the English training, the stage training ... And the next day we all came to the table, and Jimmy sat there, with his script open, and when we start, everybody closes his script again and Jimmy looks around – and closes *his* script and knew all *his* lines for the rest of rehearsal. He must have stayed up all night long.'

Stewart was ideally cast as the veteran pilot who is forever reminiscing about the days when 'flying used to be fun'. Resistant to technological change, he must take his share of the blame for the fatal crash, since he takes off without a working radio. Stewart saw the character as 'sort of a sad man in a way ... I felt he was a man who had been passed by, by the modern jet airplane and the computerized systems and automation. He wants to run the machine, he doesn't want the machine to run him.' In the midst of adversity, the backward-looking Towns comes into conflict with a German aircraft designer (Hardy Kruger), and the resulting clash between Stewart's decent conservatism and Kruger's combination of technological foresight and political ruthlessness makes for complex, absorbing drama. None of which, unfortunately, helped *The Flight of the Phoenix* at the box office, where it flopped in spectacular

Decent conservatism confronts political ruthlessness: Stewart and Hardy Kruger in THE FLIGHT OF THE PHOENIX, directed by Robert Aldrich.

Another stint in the cockpit for
The Flight of the Phoenix.

fashion: its bleak location, distended two-and-a-half-hour running time and lack of romantic interest seemed to put audiences off completely.

Three distinctly run-of-the-mill Westerns followed: *The Rare Breed* (Andrew V. McLaglen, 1966), *Firecreek* (Vincent McEveety, 1967) and *Bandolero!* (McLaglen, 1968). Of these, *Firecreek* is probably the best: a dour and somewhat pretentious return to *High Noon* territory, which gave Stewart a good rôle as the farmer and family man who also doubles as part-time sheriff and finds himself way out of his depth when a gang of desperadoes rides into town. With its gloomy musical score, its posse of unwashed, unshaven, monstrously ugly villains and its obligatory attempted-rape scene, *Firecreek* finds Hollywood starting to follow timidly in the footsteps of the Spaghetti Westerns. Stewart does his best to enter into the spirit, and at fifty-nine he gets to perform his most grisly on-screen killing when he stabs one of the bad guys through the chest with a pitchfork. His co-star was his old friend Henry Fonda, but they have hardly any scenes together, and Fonda himself realised that he had been lumbered with a thankless job. 'I played the bad guy who tried to kill Jim Stewart. Now any man who tries to kill Jim Stewart has to be marked as plain rotten. You can't get much worse than that.'

Fonda and Stewart teamed up again in 1970 for another Western, *The Cheyenne Social Club*, under the direction of Gene Kelly. This was a more relaxed, tongue-in-cheek affair about two old buddies who inherit a brothel – racy stuff, by Stewart's standards. 'It's a funny story in which a God-fearing cowboy finds himself nervously facing a situation he finds morally offensive,' he said at the time. 'Although the premise could be called bawdy, there's nothing really risqué in the film. There's some innuendo, but most of the humor is in the character and the

The swinging sixties meet the
Old West in Gene Kelly's The
Cheyenne Social Club.

situations, not in the *double entendres*.' For those in an indulgent mood the film is amusing enough, and it does convey a genuine and touching sense of the real-life friendship between the two actors.

You might think that Stewart would have enjoyed making this one, but it wasn't a happy time for him. His horse Pie (now twenty-eight years old) fell ill during the course of filming: the horse was unable to cope with the high-altitude Mexican locations, and died just ten days after Fonda – a talented watercolour artist – finished a portrait of him, which hangs in Stewart's home to this day. ('He's got a light over it now,' said Fonda. 'It's like a shrine.') More seriously, midway through the production Stewart learned that his stepson Ron had been killed while on active service in Vietnam. Fonda had to work hard to

THE CHEYENNE SOCIAL CLUB: John O'Hanlon shares the news of his inheritance with his slow-witted sidekick, Harley O'Sullivan (Henry Fonda).

An almost unrecognisable Stewart at Heathrow Airport with Gloria in 1970, en route to America for work on FOOLS' PARADE.

keep his friend's spirits up, but still there was no softening in Stewart's attitude towards the war: 'People say, what a terrible tragedy that he had to die. We never look on it as a tragedy. It's a loss, not a tragedy. He had a useful life. He graduated from college, and his country was at war. He became a Marine and when he got on the battlefield he conducted himself with gallantry. What's tragic about that? What's tragic is boys giving their lives without having a unified country behind them. That's what's tragic.'

It's clear from Stewart's uncompromising position on this issue that he was by now seriously out of step with a large body of American public opinion. Both the political and the cinematic climates of the country were going through a period of rapid change – production of his beloved Westerns had plummeted, for instance, and there was no longer any audience for them at the box office – and Stewart, despite his best efforts, was finding it impossible to adjust. His next film with Andrew V. McLaglen, *Fools' Parade*, would be his last for five years. Adapted from a novel by Davis (*The Night of the Hunter*) Grubb, it's actually quite a splendid effort, about a reformed ex-convict and his thwarted attempts to deposit his life savings in a bank. Stewart turns in a terrific performance, memorable above all for the way he keeps unscrewing his glass eye from its socket and having conversations with it. But the film did little business, and it was obvious that other avenues would have to be explored. Prior to filming *The Cheyenne Social Club* he had returned to the Broadway stage in a well-received revival of *Harvey*. Twenty-three years after he had first played Elwood P. Dowd, he was now at a much more suitable age for the rôle, and his enthusiasm for Mary Chase's unobtrusively radical fantasy remained undimmed. 'I have found, over the years,' he recalled, 'that I'll be walking down the street and someone will come up to me and say, "Is Harvey with you?" At first I would sort of joke about it. But it didn't take me long to realize that these people were not joking or making fun of it. This has happened hundreds of times, and still happens. When it does, I say, "Yes, he's right here and he gives you his best," or "No, he's home with a cold," according to the circumstances. Without fail the person will say, "The next time you see him, would you give him my best regards?" It's been a wonderful thing in my life, this big rabbit Harvey.'

Stewart also did *Harvey* on television in 1972, shortly after his series *The Jimmy Stewart Show* had been dropped after an ignominious twenty-four-week

FOOLS' PARADE: Mattie Appleyard does his disconcerting party trick.

Arthur O'Connell, William Windom and Gloria de Haven join Stewart in an episode of his short-lived series THE JIMMY STEWART SHOW.

run. It had been a gentle, well-intentioned sitcom, rather in the vein of his three 1960s comedies with Henry Koster. He had played a bumbling college professor with family problems, but the shows were lazily scripted and relied too much on expectations of audience goodwill towards the veteran star. *Hawkins on Murder*, which followed in 1973, was a series of eight ninety-minute thrillers in which Stewart starred as a lawyer loosely modelled on the Paul Biegler character in *Anatomy of a Murder*. Adequate TV slot-fillers, they failed to set the networks alight, and production was slowed down by the sixty-five year-old actor's difficulty in memorising his lines. (It was suggested that he use cue cards, but this simply created another problem: 'I can't *see* the cue cards!')

After taking *Harvey* to London in 1975, in a stage production co-starring Mona Washbourne and directed by Anthony Quayle, Stewart returned to the cinema for three cameo appearances. As Dr Hostetler in Don Siegel's *The Shootist*, he had a poignant scene with John Wayne where he had to break it to the ageing cowboy that he was dying of cancer. He took ninth billing as a multimillionaire in the disaster movie *Airport '77*, and was one of almost a dozen bemused stars roped in by Michael Winner for an utterly charmless remake of *The Big Sleep*, in which he played General Sternwood. The only link between these ill-assorted movies was that they gestured back towards, or in some way tried to reclaim, a chimerical 'Golden Age' of Hollywood cinema in which Stewart's conservative, old-fashioned values had once flourished. And his pursuit of this mirage through the desert of 1970s permissiveness would lead him, eventually, to become involved with projects that can only be described as surreal. *The Magic of Lassie*, in which he played a crusty old grandpappy, is like something out

Rehearsing the 1975 London stage production of HARVEY with director Anthony Quayle.

of Monty Python: an extraordinary musical farrago which required not only Stewart but even the dog to burst into song. *Mr Krueger's Christmas* was a thirty-minute Yuletide TV playlet showcasing the Mormon Tabernacle Choir. And finally, in what has to be one of the most bizarre codas to any Hollywood career (let alone one as distinguished as Stewart's), his last commercially released feature film was a Japanese production, *Afurika Monogatari*, shot on location in Kenya in 1979. His character has only a handful of lines and is not even given a name, while on a technical level the film is barely competent, consisting almost entirely of footage of the local wildlife interspersed with meaningless fragments of dialogue. At the end of the movie, the bearded Stewart pegs out on the floor of his hut and is buried by his granddaughter. And on this peculiar note, the cinema career of James Stewart comes to an end.

Presumably the appeal of *Afurika Monogatari* (also known as *The Green Horizon*) lay in its location and its environmental subject matter. Spurred on largely by his daughter Kelly, who has become heavily involved in wildlife issues, Stewart has lately emerged as something of a spokesman for the conservation lobby, having narrated a documentary (*We Call Them Brother*, 1973), been a judge at the World Wildlife Fund's film and TV festival in Bristol, and made numerous trips to India and Africa (although not as a hunter, as he once did). It seems a natural extension of his rôle as honoured patriarch and elder statesman, which has been filling his time very satisfactorily since he retired from the screen. In this capacity, he has been required to turn up at the occasional Hollywood function to collect an honorary Oscar or an American Film Institute Life Achievement Award or to be fêted by the Film Society of Lincoln Center; he has been a guest of honour at dinners given by President Reagan, always on hand to provide a

Below: A valedictory appearance with old friend (and political soulmate) John Wayne in Don Siegel's THE SHOOTIST.
Bottom: Sharing a poignant moment with Stephanie Zimbalist in THE MAGIC OF LASSIE. The dog looks happy, perhaps because he's the only one who hasn't seen the script.

Still sporting his FOOLS' PARADE moustache, Stewart signs autographs for an audience which looks far too young to have seen any of his most famous films.

rousing tribute to the latter's policy achievements (Stewart was also a close friend of the Nixons, although that seemed to cool off a little after Watergate). He has been an outspoken opponent of colourisation, which he repeatedly condemns as an act of cultural vandalism whenever he can find a platform; he has received further military honours, such as the Medal of Freedom in 1985, and has served as an Elder of the Beverly Hills Community Presbyterian Church, a member of the Los Angeles Boy Scout Council and one of the Board of Directors of Project Hope, a building scheme for the homeless. And, more lucratively, he has become known in America as the voice of Campbell's soup, after a series of TV adverts for which he provided the homely voice-over, and has established himself as a bestselling author with a slim volume of ingratiating verse called *Jimmy Stewart and His Poems*.

There have been some fleeting returns to acting. In 1982, plans were announced to cast Stewart as a local doctor who doubles as small-town mayor in a TV series called *His Honor, Doc Potter*. It never happened (and perhaps we should be grateful), but the next year he did co-star with Bette Davis in *Right of Way*, an over-earnest TV movie about euthanasia. In 1986 he took a small part in *North and South: Book Two*, but he has been kept off the screen since then by a combination of health problems and the general dearth of worthwhile opportunities for the senior actor. In 1993 he was candid enough to admit, 'I don't like the way I've grown old. I don't like my looks.' And so, although he was happy to provide one of the cartoon voices for *An American Tail: Fievel Goes West*, the word now seems to be that James Stewart is no longer available. To use his own phrase: 'I think I've done enough.'

'I think I've done enough': it is, when you think about it, an astonishingly modest understatement. The truth is that no actor ever did more than Stewart to embody the often contradictory spirit of his country and give it convincing expression on screen. He could have been a soldier, he could have been an architect, he could have been an aeronautical engineer, but chance decreed that he would finally devote himself to acting – the art of wrestling with reality. Once that had happened, commitment

Stewart's last piece of screen work to date: voicing the part of 'Wylie Burp' in AN AMERICAN TAIL: FIEVEL GOES WEST.

to excellence within his field became Stewart's governing ideal, and like Destry with his postage stamp, he stuck to it. It's a long time now since he made a film, and an even longer time since he made a really good one. But between his earliest movies at MGM and his last serious feature-film rôle in 1971, we have thirty-five years of the most honest, dedicated and adventurous screen acting that Hollywood is ever likely to give us. Stewart himself is never likely to make the boast, so let Elwood P. Dowd now do it for him: 'I've wrestled with reality for thirty-five years, doctor, and I'm happy to state that I finally won out over it.'

Demonstrating his commitment to wildlife issues for the benefit of interviewer Barbara Walters.

As Teddy Dwyer in the TV movie Right of Way *(1983) – his last major dramatic rôle and his first ever appearance opposite Bette Davis.*

Feature Films

1935 The Murder Man

1936 Rose Marie
Next Time We Love
Wife vs. Secretary
Small Town Girl
Speed
The Gorgeous Hussy
Born to Dance
After the Thin Man

1937 Seventh Heaven
The Last Gangster
Navy Blue and Gold

1938 Of Human Hearts
Vivacious Lady
The Shopworn Angel
You Can't Take It with You

1939 Made for Each Other
The Ice Follies of 1939
It's a Wonderful World
Mr Smith Goes to Washington
Destry Rides Again

1940 The Shop around the Corner
The Mortal Storm
No Time for Comedy
The Philadelphia Story

1941 Come Live with Me
Pot O' Gold/The Golden Hour
Ziegfeld Girl

1947 It's a Wonderful Life
Magic Town

1948 On Our Merry Way
Call Northside 777
Rope
You Gotta Stay Happy

1949 The Stratton Story
Malaya

1950 Winchester '73
Broken Arrow
The Jackpot
Harvey

1951 No Highway

1952 The Greatest Show on Earth
Bend of the River/Where the
River Bends
Carbine Williams
The Naked Spur

1953 Thunder Bay
The Glenn Miller Story

1954 Rear Window

1955 The Far Country
Strategic Air Command
The Man from Laramie

1956 The Man Who Knew Too Much

1957 The Spirit of St Louis
Night Passage

1958 Vertigo
Bell, Book and Candle

1959 Anatomy of a Murder
The FBI Story

1960 The Mountain Road

1961 Two Rode Together

1962 The Man Who Shot Liberty Valance
Mr Hobbs Takes a Vacation
How the West Was Won

1963 Take Her, She's Mine

1964 Cheyenne Autumn

1965 Dear Brigitte
Shenandoah
The Flight of the Phoenix

1966 The Rare Breed

1968 Firecreek
Bandolero!

1970 The Cheyenne Social Club

1971 Fools' Parade/Dynamite Man from
Glory Jail

1976 The Shootist

1977 Airport '77

1978 The Big Sleep
The Magic of Lassie

1981 The Green Horizon/Afurika Monogatari

1990 An American Tail: Fievel Goes West

Shorts, Documentaries and Narrations

Art Trouble (1934)

Important News (1936)

Fellow Americans (1942)

Winning Your Wings (1942)

The American Creed (1946)

Thunderbolt (1947)

10,000 Kids and a Cop (1948)

How Much Do You Owe? (1949)

And Then There Were Four (1950)

Ambassadors with Wings (1958)

X15 (1961)

Pat Nixon: Portrait of a First Lady (1972)

We Call Them Brother (1973)

That's Entertainment! (1974)

Sentimental Journey (1976)

Television

The Windmill (1955)

The Town with a Past (1957)

The Trail to Christmas (1957)

Cindy's Fella (1959)

Flashing Spikes (1962)

The Jimmy Stewart Show (1971)

Harvey (1972)

Hawkins on Murder (1973)

Mr Krueger's Christmas (1981)

Right of Way (1983)

North and South: Book Two (1986)